taste of home breakfast

WAKE UP
YOUR TASTE BUDS
WITH 235
DAYBREAK DISHES

Ever wonder why breakfast is called the most important meal of the day? Taste for yourself with any of the sunrise favorites in *Taste of Home Breakfast.*

Indulge in a stack of fluffy pancakes drenched in rich, buttery syrup, golden waffles topped with whipped cream and fruit, hearty omelets stuffed with farm-fresh ingredients, crumbly coffee cakes drizzled with sweet icing and more. *Taste of Home Breakfast* serves over 230 eye-opening recipes guaranteed to start the day right.

Featuring traditional breakfast staples, as well as delectable new creations, this colorful book lets you enjoy all the favorites of your local pancake house at your own kitchen table. Eight mouthwatering chapters—Brunch Classics; Eye-Opening Eggs; Pancakes & Crepes; Waffles & French Toast; Breakfast To Go; Kids' Weekend Favorites; Special Occasion Breakfasts; and Breads & Sweet Treats—let you savor the best part of the day, one bite at a time.

When you need a something quick before rushing out the door, hearty Sausage Omelet Bagels (p. 65) and refreshing Banana Coffee Smoothies (p. 58) will fill you up without slowing you down. If you've decided to kick back and enjoy a leisurely brunch with friends, you can't go wrong with luscious Creamy Rhubarb Crepes (p. 32) or heaping helpings of Smoked Sausage Scramble (p. 22).

When the occasion calls for something that'll make the day dazzle, turn to more exciting creations such as delicious Fruit-Filled Puff Pancake (p. 87), savory Crab-Spinach Egg Casserole (p. 86) and impressive Chicken Cordon Bleu Crepes (p. 86).

Thanks to everyday ingredients, easy-to-follow instructions, handy cooking tips and enticing full-color photos, the recipes inside *Taste of Home Breakfast* are destined to find a place among your most treasured morning mainstays for years to come.

taste of home.
breakfast

Senior Vice President, Editor in Chief:	Catherine Cassidy
Vice President, Executive Editor/Books:	Heidi Reuter Lloyd
Creative Director:	Ardyth Cope
Food Director:	Diane Werner RD
Senior Editor/Books:	Mark Hagen
Editor:	Sara Lancaster
Art Director:	Rudy Krochalk
Content Production Supervisor:	Julie Wagner
Layout Designer:	Nancy Novak
Proofreaders:	Linne Bruskewitz, Amy Glander
Recipe Asset Management System:	Coleen Martin, Sue A. Jurack
Premedia Supervisor:	Scott Berger
Recipe Testing and Editing:	Taste of Home Test Kitchen
Food Photography:	Reiman Photo Studio
Editorial Assistant:	Barb Czysz
Cover Photo Photographer:	Rob Hagen
Cover Photo Set Stylist:	Dolores Jacq
Cover Photo Food Stylist:	Kaitlyn Besasie
Chief Marketing Officer:	Lisa Karpinski
Vice President/Book Marketing:	Dan Fink
Creative Director/Creative Marketing:	Jim Palmen

The Reader's Digest Association, Inc.

President and Chief Executive Officer:	Tom Williams
Executive Vice President, RDA, and President, North America:	Dan Lagani

International Standard Book Number (10): 0-89821-760-1
International Standard Book Number (13): 978-0-89821-760-5
Library of Congress Control Number: 2009931202

Timeless Recipes from Trusted Home Cooks®
is a registered trademark of Reiman Media Group, Inc.

Pictured on front cover: Bacon Vegetable Quiche (p. 22)

Pictured on title page: Blueberry Sour Cream Pancakes (p. 31)

Pictured on back cover: Peach Cobbler Coffee Cake (p. 97),
Puffy Oven Pancakes (p. 40), Mini Ham 'n' Cheese Frittatas (p. 19)

PAGE 58

PAGE 5

PAGE 98

TABLE OF CONTENTS

GREAT GIFTS!

BRUNCH CLASSICS

GATHER WITH FRIENDS TO WELCOME THE WEEKEND IN GOOD TASTE WITH THESE ENTICING BRUNCH SPECIALTIES.

CHICKEN 'N' HAM FRITTATA
PAGE 8

Breakfast TIP

Extra crescent rolls can be a great addition to your brunch gathering. Lightly spritz the rolls with butter-flavored spray or nonstick cooking spray. Then sprinkle each with sugar and cinnamon and microwave for 15 to 20 seconds. Placed in a bread basket, the warm, sweet bundles are a delicious surprise to your brunch menu.

—Robin T.
Los Gatos, California

BACON QUICHE TARTS

Flavored with vegetables, cheese and bacon, these memorable morsels are bound to be a frequent request at your house. The tarts are guaranteed to impress, but surprisingly simple to make.

kendra schertz | nappanee, indiana

BACON QUICHE TARTS
YIELD: 8 SERVINGS

2 packages (3 ounces *each*) cream cheese, softened
5 teaspoons milk
2 eggs
1/2 cup shredded Colby cheese
2 tablespoons chopped green pepper
1 tablespoon finely chopped onion
1 tube (8 ounces) refrigerated crescent rolls
5 bacon strips, cooked and crumbled

In a small bowl, beat cream cheese and milk until smooth. Add the eggs, cheese, green pepper and onion; mix well.

Separate the crescent roll dough into eight triangles; press onto the bottom and up the sides of greased muffin cups. Sprinkle half of the bacon into cups. Pour egg mixture over bacon; top with remaining bacon. Bake, uncovered, at 375° for 18-22 minutes or until a knife comes out clean. Serve warm.

HINT OF MINT FRUIT SALAD

I love making herbal syrups like the simple dressing I use on this colorful fruit salad. It definitely adds pizzazz to an ordinary brunch.

sue gronholz | beaver dam, wisconsin

HINT OF MINT FRUIT SALAD
YIELD: 12 SERVINGS

1	cup sugar
1	cup water
1	cup loosely packed mint sprigs
2-1/2	cups chopped apples
2-1/2	cups chopped ripe pears
2	cups cubed fresh pineapple
2	cups sliced fresh strawberries
1	cup fresh blueberries
1	cup mayonnaise

In a large saucepan, bring sugar and water to a boil. Reduce heat; simmer, uncovered, for 4 minutes. Remove from the heat. Add mint; cover and steep for 20 minutes. Strain and discard mint. Transfer syrup to a small bowl; refrigerate until chilled.

Just before serving, combine the apples, pears, pineapple, strawberries and blueberries in a large bowl. Stir mayonnaise into mint syrup until blended; pour over fruit and toss to coat.

AVOCADO EGGS BENEDICT
YIELD: 6 SERVINGS

1/2	cup butter
1/4	cup all-purpose flour
2	cups milk
2	cups (8 ounces) shredded cheddar cheese
1	tablespoon grated Romano cheese
1/2	teaspoon salt
1/8	teaspoon garlic powder
1/8	teaspoon dried thyme
1/8	teaspoon *each* ground mustard, coriander and pepper
1	tablespoon white vinegar
6	eggs
6	slices Canadian bacon, warmed
1	large ripe avocado, peeled and sliced
3	English muffins, split and toasted

In a large saucepan, melt butter. Stir in flour until smooth; gradually add milk. Bring to a boil; cook and stir for 2 minutes or until thickened. Reduce heat; stir in the cheeses and seasonings. Cook and stir until cheese is melted; keep warm.

Place 2-3 in. of water in a large skillet with high sides; add vinegar. Bring to a boil; reduce heat and simmer gently. Break cold eggs, one at a time, into a custard cup or saucer; holding the cup close to the surface of the water, slip each egg into water. Cook, uncovered, until whites are completely set and yolks begin to thicken (but are not hard), about 4 minutes.

Place Canadian bacon and avocado on each muffin half. With a slotted spoon, lift each egg out of the water and place over avocado. Top egg with cheese sauce.

AVOCADO EGGS BENEDICT

Fresh avocado slices and a creamy sauce really dress up this classic egg dish. It's great for special-occasion meals.

deborah, doug and jory hilpipre | eden prairie, minnesota

CAJUN-STYLE BRUNCH BAKE

CAJUN-STYLE BRUNCH BAKE
YIELD: 6 SERVINGS

It's so handy to fix this hearty breakfast casserole the night before and refrigerate it until morning. It was given to me by a co-worker and has turned out to be a family hit. I adapted it to our tastes, adding onion, potato and Cajun seasoning.

kathie deusser | church point, louisiana

- 6 eggs, lightly beaten
- 2 cups milk
- 1 pound sliced bacon, cooked and crumbled
- 6 slices bread, cubed
- 1 medium potato, peeled and diced
- 1 cup (4 ounces) shredded cheddar cheese
- 1/2 cup finely chopped onion
- 1 to 1-1/2 teaspoons Cajun seasoning
- 1 teaspoon salt

In a large bowl, combine all ingredients. Transfer to a greased 11-in. x 7-in. baking dish. Cover and refrigerate overnight.

Remove from the refrigerator 30 minutes before baking. Bake, uncovered, at 350° for 45-50 minutes or until a knife inserted near the center comes out clean. Let casserole stand for 10 minutes before cutting.

GLAZED BACON
YIELD: 8 SERVINGS

Brown sugar, Dijon mustard and wine make bacon a little more unique in this recipe. The popular side is easy to prepare while working on the rest of the morning meal.

judith dobson | burlington, wisconsin

- 1 pound sliced bacon
- 1 cup packed brown sugar
- 1/4 cup white wine *or* unsweetened apple juice
- 2 tablespoons Dijon mustard

Place bacon on a rack in an ungreased 15-in. x 10-in. baking pan. Bake at 350° for 10 minutes; drain.

Combine the brown sugar, wine or juice and mustard; drizzle half over bacon. Bake for 10 minutes. Turn bacon and drizzle with remaining glaze. Bake 10 minutes longer or until golden brown. Place bacon on waxed paper until set. Serve warm.

CHICKEN CLUB BRUNCH RING
YIELD: 16 SERVINGS

A few tubes of crescent rolls make this impressive recipe a snap. I fill the ring with a flavorful chicken salad and serve warm slices with a mustard-flavored mayonnaise.

rebecca clark | warrior, alabama

- 1/2 cup mayonnaise
- 1 tablespoon minced fresh parsley
- 2 teaspoons Dijon mustard
- 1-1/2 teaspoons finely chopped onion
- 1-3/4 cups cubed cooked chicken breast (1/2-inch cubes)
- 2 bacon strips, cooked and crumbled
- 1 cup (4 ounces) shredded Swiss cheese, *divided*
- 2 tubes (8 ounces *each*) refrigerated crescent rolls
- 2 plum tomatoes
- 2 cups shredded lettuce

In a large bowl, combine the mayonnaise, parsley, mustard and onion. Stir in the chicken, bacon and 3/4 cup cheese. Unroll crescent dough; separate into 16 triangles. Arrange on an ungreased 12-in. round pizza pan, forming a ring with pointed ends facing outer edge of pan and wide ends overlapping.

Spoon chicken mixture over wide ends; fold points over filling and tuck under wide ends (filling will be visible). Chop half of a tomato; set aside. Slice remaining tomatoes; place over filling and tuck into dough.

Bake at 375° for 20-25 minutes or until golden brown. Sprinkle with remaining cheese. Let stand for 5 minutes. Place lettuce in center of ring; sprinkle with chopped tomato.

CHICKEN CLUB BRUNCH RING

BRUNCH PUFFS MAIN DISH
YIELD: 8 SERVINGS

*This recipe wasn't handed down from my mother—
it was passed "up" from my granddaughter! It's now a favorite
dish at my home for Mother's Day and at other celebrations.*

judy gochenour | logan, iowa

1	cup water
1/2	cup butter
1/2	teaspoon salt
1	cup all-purpose flour
4	eggs

FILLING:

1/2	cup chopped green pepper
1/2	cup chopped onion
1	tablespoon butter
8	eggs
1/2	teaspoon salt
1/4	teaspoon pepper
1	cup chopped fully cooked ham
1	cup (4 ounces) shredded cheddar cheese

In a large saucepan, bring water, butter and salt to a boil. Add flour all at once and stir until a smooth ball forms. Remove from the heat; let stand 5 minutes. Add eggs, one at a time, beating well after each addition. Beat until mixture is smooth and shiny.

Drop batter by 1/4 cupfuls 2 in. apart onto a greased baking sheet. Bake at 400° for 35 minutes or until golden brown. Transfer puffs to a wire rack. Immediately split puffs open; remove and discard tops and soft dough from inside. Set hollowed-out puffs aside.

In a large skillet, saute green pepper and onion in butter until tender. In a medium bowl, beat eggs, salt and pepper. Add to skillet, stirring over medium heat until almost done. Add ham and cheddar cheese; stir until eggs are set. Spoon egg mixture into puffs. Serve immediately.

ASPARAGUS WITH ORANGE BUTTER

ASPARAGUS WITH ORANGE BUTTER
YIELD: 4 SERVINGS

Our home economists use a simple orange butter to enhance the natural great taste of asparagus. This side is a wonderful addition to any spring brunch.

taste of home test kitchen

3	tablespoons butter, softened
1	tablespoon thawed orange juice concentrate
1/2	teaspoon grated orange peel
1/8	teaspoon onion powder
1/8	teaspoon Dijon mustard
1/2	cup water
1	pound fresh asparagus, trimmed

Salt to taste

In a small bowl, combine the first five ingredients until blended. In a large skillet, bring water to a boil. Add asparagus; cover and boil for 3-4 minutes or until tender. Drain and set aside.

In the same skillet, melt butter mixture, then add asparagus and toss to coat. Sprinkle with salt.

CHICKEN 'N' HAM FRITTATA
YIELD: 6 SERVINGS

Because my group is on the go, we often gather for Sunday brunch to discuss plans for the upcoming week while enjoying servings of this hearty egg dish. It's colorful and even special enough to prepare for our holiday get-togethers, too.

ruth allen | hebron, kentucky

1/2	cup chopped green onions
2	garlic cloves, minced
2	tablespoons canola oil
1-1/4	cups chopped yellow summer squash

BRUNCH PUFFS MAIN DISH

- 1 cup chopped zucchini
- 1/2 cup chopped sweet yellow pepper
- 1/2 cup chopped sweet red pepper
- 1 teaspoon minced fresh gingerroot
- 2 cups cubed cooked chicken breast
- 1 cup chopped deli ham
- 6 eggs
- 3/4 cup mayonnaise
- 1/4 teaspoon prepared horseradish
- 1/4 teaspoon pepper
- 1 cup (4 ounces) shredded Monterey Jack cheese

In a large ovenproof skillet, saute the onions and garlic in oil for 1 minute. Add the yellow squash, zucchini, peppers and ginger. Cook and stir for 8 minutes or until vegetables are crisp-tender. Add the chicken and ham; cook 1 minute longer or until heated through. Remove from the heat.

In a large bowl, whisk the eggs, mayonnaise, horseradish and pepper until blended. Pour into skillet. Bake, uncovered, at 350° for 25-30 minutes or until eggs are completely set. Sprinkle with cheese; cover and let stand for 5 minutes or until cheese is melted.

CHICKEN 'N' HAM FRITTATA

NEW POTATOES WITH DILL
YIELD: 4 SERVINGS

Even though these spuds are quick and easy to make, the potatoes look delightful and taste wonderful, especially when paired with ham for an Easter brunch.

lorene frohling | waukesha, wisconsin

- 1 pound unpeeled new potatoes, julienned
- 2 tablespoons butter
- 1 teaspoon snipped fresh dill *or* 1/2 teaspoon dill weed
- 1/2 teaspoon seasoned salt

In a greased 11-in. x 7-in. baking dish, arrange potatoes in a single layer. Dot with butter; sprinkle with dill and salt. Cover and bake at 425° for 20-25 minutes or until tender, stirring once.

CHEDDAR HAM STRATA

CHEDDAR HAM STRATA
YIELD: 12 SERVINGS

I put together this ham and egg dish on Christmas Eve and refrigerate it. Then, while we open presents on Christmas morning, I pop it into the oven for breakfast. It's now a family tradition.

ann pool | jerome, idaho

- 10 slices day-old bread, crusts removed and cubed
- 1 medium onion, finely chopped
- 4 medium fresh mushrooms, finely chopped
- 1/4 cup butter, cubed
- 4 cups (16 ounces) shredded cheddar cheese
- 2 cups cubed fully cooked ham
- 2 tablespoons all-purpose flour
- 8 eggs
- 3 cups milk
- 2 tablespoons prepared mustard
- 1 teaspoon garlic powder
- 1/2 teaspoon salt

Place the bread cubes in a greased 13-in. x 9-in. baking dish. In a small skillet, saute onion and mushrooms in butter; spoon over bread. Sprinkle with cheese, ham and flour. In a large bowl, whisk the eggs, milk, mustard, garlic powder and salt. Pour over ham and cheese. Cover and refrigerate overnight.

Remove from the refrigerator 30 minutes before baking. Bake, uncovered, at 350° for 60-70 minutes or until a knife inserted near the center comes out clean. Let stand for 10 minutes before serving.

Breakfast TIP

Once a loaf of bread is down to the last few slices, I cube it, put it in a freezer bag and place in the freezer. Then I have bread crumbs ready to go when I need them.

—*Helen R., Rockton, Illinois*

SHEPHERD'S INN BREAKFAST PIE
YIELD: 6 SERVINGS

Running a bed-and-breakfast keeps us busy. This quick-to-fix morning casserole is a favorite among our guests.

ellen berdan | salkum, washington

1-1/2	pounds bulk pork sausage
4	cups frozen Tater Tots
1	cup (4 ounces) shredded cheddar cheese
4	eggs
1/2	cup milk
1	tablespoon minced green onion
1/8	teaspoon pepper

Dash garlic powder

Minced chives

2	tomatoes, sliced and quartered

In a large skillet, cook sausage over medium heat until no longer pink; drain. Spread in an ungreased 11-in. x 7-in. baking dish. Top with Tater Tots; sprinkle with cheese.

In a bowl, beat eggs, milk, onion, pepper and garlic powder just until blended. Pour over cheese. Cover; bake at 350° for 30 minutes. Uncover; bake 20-25 minutes longer. Sprinkle with chives. Top with tomatoes.

HOT FRUIT AND SAUSAGE
YIELD: 6 SERVINGS

The flavor of pineapple and banana is a delicious complement to the savory sausage links. Brown sugar and a dash of cinnamon add a delightful touch that's sure to please.

marian peterson | wisconsin rapids, wisconsin

1	package (12 ounces) uncooked pork sausage links
3/4	cup pineapple tidbits
2	tablespoons brown sugar

Pinch ground cinnamon

1	medium firm banana, sliced

In a large skillet, cook the sausage links according to package directions; drain. Add the pineapple tidbits, brown sugar and cinnamon; heat through. Stir in sliced banana just before serving.

RED PEPPER CORNMEAL SOUFFLE
YIELD: 8-10 SERVINGS

I use the vegetables from our garden in all my cooking. Doing so adds from-scratch flavor that just can't be beat. Dotted with parsley and red pepper, this beautiful souffle is a wonderful brunch dish.

janet eckhoff | woodland, california

1	large onion, chopped
1	cup chopped sweet red pepper
1/4	cup butter
3	cups milk
2/3	cup cornmeal
1	cup (4 ounces) shredded sharp cheddar cheese
2	tablespoons minced fresh parsley
1	teaspoon salt, *divided*
1/2	teaspoon white pepper
2	egg yolks, beaten
7	egg whites
1/2	teaspoon cream of tartar

In a large saucepan, saute the onion and red pepper in butter until tender. Add the milk. Bring to a boil. Gradually whisk in cornmeal; whisk constantly until thickened, about 5 minutes. Add the cheese, parsley, 1/2 teaspoon salt and pepper. Add 1 cup of the cornmeal mixture to the egg yolks; mix well. Return all to saucepan.

In a large bowl, beat egg whites, cream of tartar and remaining salt until stiff peaks form. Fold into the cornmeal mixture. Transfer to a greased 2-qt. souffle dish. Bake at 375° for 35-40 minutes or until golden brown.

RED PEPPER CORNMEAL SOUFFLE

STEAK HASH
YIELD: 4 SERVINGS

You can give leftover steak and baked potatoes a flavorful face-lift with this idea. Green pepper, onion and garlic powder lend just enough seasoning to the easy a.m. specialty.

barbara nowakowski | north tonawanda, new york

1	medium green pepper, chopped
1	small onion, chopped
2	tablespoons canola oil
3	medium potatoes (about 1 pound), peeled, cooked and diced
1	cooked steak, diced (about 1 cup)
1/4	to 1/2 teaspoon garlic powder

Salt and pepper to taste

1/4	cup shredded Monterey Jack cheese
4	eggs

In a large skillet, saute the green pepper and onion in oil until tender. Stir in potatoes. Reduce heat; cover and cook over low heat for 10 minutes or until the potatoes are heated through, stirring occasionally.

Add steak, garlic powder, salt and pepper. Sprinkle with cheese. Cover and cook on low 5 minutes longer or until heated through and cheese is melted; keep warm. Prepare eggs as desired. Divide hash among four plates and top with an egg.

UPSIDE-DOWN BREAKFAST
YIELD: 4 SERVINGS

I first sampled this baked entree at my mother-in-law's and knew immediately I wanted the recipe. Pineapple and brown sugar add a touch of sweetness to the rice and ham.

tracy mc dowell | moose jaw, saskatchewan

3	tablespoons butter, melted
3	tablespoons brown sugar
1	can (8 ounces) sliced pineapple, drained
2	slices fully cooked ham (6-1/4 inches x 4-1/2 inches x 1/2 inch)
1-1/2	cups uncooked instant rice
1	cup milk
1	cup water
2	tablespoons plus 1-1/2 teaspoons all-purpose flour
1-1/2	teaspoons dried minced onion
1/2	teaspoon salt
1/8	teaspoon pepper

In an ungreased 11-in. x 7-in. baking dish, combine butter and brown sugar. Arrange pineapple slices and ham on top. In a saucepan over medium heat, combine remaining ingredients; bring to a boil. Reduce heat; cover and simmer, stirring occasionally, for 5 minutes or until rice is tender. Spread over ham.

Bake, uncovered, at 400° for 10 minutes. Let stand for 3 minutes. Invert onto a serving platter and let stand for 1 minute before removing baking dish.

MIXED BERRY FRENCH TOAST BAKE

MIXED BERRY FRENCH TOAST BAKE
YIELD: 8 SERVINGS

I love this recipe! Perfect for fuss-free holiday meals or overnight company, it's scrumptious and so effortless to pull together the night before.

amy berry | poland, maine

1	loaf (1 pound) French bread, cubed
6	egg whites
3	eggs
1-3/4	cups fat-free milk
1	teaspoon sugar
1	teaspoon ground cinnamon
1	teaspoon vanilla extract
1/4	teaspoon salt
1	package (12 ounces) frozen unsweetened mixed berries
2	tablespoons cold butter
1/3	cup packed brown sugar

Place bread cubes in a 13-in. x 9-in. baking dish coated with cooking spray. In a large bowl, combine the egg whites, eggs, milk, sugar, cinnamon, vanilla and salt; pour over bread. Cover and refrigerate for 8 hours or overnight.

Thirty minutes before baking, remove the berries from the freezer and set aside; remove baking dish from the refrigerator. Bake, covered, at 350° for 30 minutes.

In a small bowl, cut butter into brown sugar until crumbly. Sprinkle berries and brown sugar mixture over French toast. Bake, uncovered, for 15-20 minutes or until a knife inserted near the center comes out clean.

CHICKEN A LA KING

CHICKEN A LA KING
YIELD: 4 SERVINGS

Canned soup makes this elegant classic so quick and easy, while pimientos, celery and peppers add both color and crunch. It's a great recipe for using up leftover chicken.

jennifer eggebraaten | *delton, michigan*

- 1/2 cup chopped celery
- 1/2 cup chopped green pepper
- 2 tablespoons butter
- 2 cans (10-3/4 ounces *each*) condensed cream of chicken soup, undiluted
- 1 cup milk
- 1/4 teaspoon pepper
- 2 cups cubed cooked chicken
- 1 jar (6 ounces) sliced mushrooms, drained
- 1/4 cup diced pimientos
- 6 slices bread, toasted and halved

In a large skillet, saute celery and green pepper in butter until crisp-tender. Stir in the soup, milk and pepper. Add the chicken, mushrooms and pimientos. Reduce heat; simmer, uncovered, for 4-6 minutes or until heated through. Serve over toast.

CHILI 'N' CHEESE GRITS
YIELD: 6-8 SERVINGS

Although I live in a big city, I'm really a country cook. Most of our friends laugh about my love of grits, but there are never any leftovers from this recipe.

rosemary west | *las vegas, nevada*

- 2 cups water
- 2 cups milk
- 1 cup grits
- 2 egg yolks

- 1 cup (4 ounces) shredded cheddar cheese, *divided*
- 1/4 cup butter, cubed
- 1 can (4 ounces) chopped green chilies, drained
- 1 teaspoon salt

In a large saucepan, bring water and milk to a boil. Add grits; cook and stir over medium heat for 5 minutes or until thickened.

In a small bowl, beat egg yolks. Stir a small amount of hot grits into egg yolks; mix well. Return all to the pan, stirring constantly. Add 3/4 cup shredded cheddar cheese, butter, green chilies and salt. Pour mixture into a greased 1-1/2-qt. baking dish. Sprinkle with the remaining cheese. Bake, uncovered, at 350° for 30-35 minutes or until golden brown.

SPICED TOMATO JUICE

SPICED TOMATO JUICE
YIELD: 8 SERVINGS (ABOUT 2 QUARTS)

I always serve this spiced-up tomato juice at our family's Easter Sunday brunch, but it's good with any special occasion meal throughout the year.

mary selner | *green bay, wisconsin*

- 2 cans (32 ounces *each*) tomato juice
- 1/2 cup lemon juice
- 1/4 cup lime juice
- 2 tablespoons Worcestershire sauce
- 1 to 1-1/2 teaspoons pepper
- 1 teaspoon salt
- 1/8 to 1/4 teaspoon hot pepper sauce
- 8 medium celery ribs with leaves

In a large pitcher, combine the first seven ingredients; stir well. Pour into glasses. Garnish with celery. Serve immediately.

SCRAMBLED EGG MUFFINS
YIELD: 1 DOZEN

After enjoying scrambled egg muffins at a local restaurant, I came up with this savory version that my husband likes even better. People love the unique presentation of a brunch classic.

cathy larkins | marshfield, missouri

1/2	pound bulk pork sausage
12	eggs
1/2	cup chopped onion
1/4	cup chopped green pepper
1/2	teaspoon salt
1/4	teaspoon pepper
1/4	teaspoon garlic powder
1/2	cup shredded cheddar cheese

In a large skillet, cook the sausage over medium heat until no longer pink; drain. In a large bowl, beat the eggs. Add the onion, green pepper, salt, pepper and garlic powder. Stir in sausage and cheese.

Spoon by 1/3 cupfuls into greased muffin cups. Bake at 350° for 20-25 minutes or until a knife inserted near the center comes out clean.

SCRAMBLED EGG MUFFINS

TURKEY SAUSAGE PATTIES
YIELD: 6 SERVINGS

Everybody who samples this breakfast sausage raves about the taste and is amazed to learn it's made of ground turkey. I like knowing I am serving friends and family something they love that is good for them, too!

sally brassfield | california, maryland

2	to 3 teaspoons rubbed sage
1	teaspoon brown sugar
1/4	teaspoon crushed red pepper flakes
1/4	teaspoon ground nutmeg
1/4	teaspoon pepper
Pinch	allspice
1	pound lean ground turkey

In a bowl, combine the first six ingredients. Add turkey; mix until combined. Shape into six patties. Lightly coat a skillet with cooking spray. Cook the sausage patties over medium heat until browned on both sides and the meat is no longer pink, about 15-20 minutes.

CORNMEAL HAM CAKES

CORNMEAL HAM CAKES
YIELD: 4 SERVINGS

These hearty cakes are great for breakfast, but my husband and I also enjoy their delicious cornmeal flavor for supper. The pineapple-maple syrup provides a flavor that perfectly complements the pieces of ham tucked into each hotcake.

priscilla gilbert | indian harbour beach, florida

1/2	cup all-purpose flour
1/2	cup cornmeal
2	tablespoons sugar
1/2	teaspoon baking powder
1/4	teaspoon baking soda
1/8	teaspoon salt
2	eggs, lightly beaten
1	cup buttermilk
3	tablespoons butter, melted
1	teaspoon vanilla extract
1-1/2	cups diced fully cooked ham

PINEAPPLE MAPLE SYRUP:

1	cup diced fresh pineapple
1/4	teaspoon ground cinnamon
1	tablespoon butter
1	cup maple syrup

In a large bowl, combine the first six ingredients. Combine the eggs, buttermilk, butter and vanilla; stir into dry ingredients until well blended. Fold in ham. Pour batter by 1/4 cupfuls onto a greased hot griddle. Turn when bubbles form on top; cook until second side is golden brown.

For syrup, in a small saucepan, saute pineapple and cinnamon in butter for 4-6 minutes or until pineapple is browned. Stir in maple syrup. Serve with pancakes.

SCRAMBLED EGG SANDWICH

YIELD: 6 SERVINGS

Frozen garlic bread makes for a deliciously different breakfast sandwich. Scrambled eggs and sliced mozzarella are placed between two hearty slices for a mouth-watering bite.

kim dunbar | willow springs, illinois

1	loaf (16 ounces) frozen garlic bread, thawed
1/2	cup finely chopped onion
1/2	cup finely chopped green pepper
3	tablespoons butter
10	eggs
1/4	cup milk

Salt and pepper to taste

6	to 8 slices part-skim mozzarella cheese

Bake garlic bread according to package directions. Meanwhile, in a large skillet, saute onion and green pepper in butter until crisp-tender. In a large bowl, whisk the eggs, milk, salt and pepper. Pour into skillet; cook and stir over medium heat until eggs are completely set. Remove from the heat and keep warm.

Arrange cheese slices on bottom half of bread; spoon eggs over cheese. Replace bread top. Slice and serve immediately.

SCRAMBLED EGG SANDWICH

POTATO LEEK SKILLET

YIELD: 4 SERVINGS

Before sampling this recipe from a neighbor, I never had eaten leeks. I've since fallen in love with their mellow, slightly sweet flavor. This is a nice option for a Sunday brunch.

sharon boyajian | linden, california

1/2	pound ground beef
2	medium potatoes, cubed and cooked
3	large leeks (white part only), cut into 1/2-inch slices
1/2	cup water
2	tablespoons olive oil
1	teaspoon salt

1/2	teaspoon pepper
1/2	teaspoon dill weed

In a skillet, cook beef over medium heat until no longer pink; drain. Add the potatoes, leeks, water, oil, salt, pepper and dill. Bring to a boil. Reduce heat; simmer, uncovered, until leeks are tender, about 5 minutes.

EDITOR'S NOTE: Leeks are part of the onion family and resemble a large green onion. Sand is often found between their many layers. So if a leek is to be sliced, cut it open lengthwise down one side and rinse under cold running water, separating the leaves.

TOMATO AND CHEESE STRATA

YIELD: 4-6 SERVINGS

This is a great make-ahead dish. Brimming with fresh tomatoes and cheddar cheese, it's absolutely delicious! People who try it always ask me for the recipe.

molly seidel | edgewood, new mexico

10	slices white bread
4	medium tomatoes, sliced 1/2 inch thick
1	cup (4 ounces) shredded cheddar cheese
4	green onions, thinly sliced
4	eggs
2	cups milk
1/2	teaspoon salt

Line a greased 8-in. square baking dish with four bread slices. Layer with half of the tomatoes, cheese and onions. Top with remaining bread (slices will overlap). Layer with remaining tomatoes, cheese and onions.

In a small bowl, whisk the eggs, milk and salt. Pour over the top. Cover and refrigerate overnight.

Remove from the refrigerator 30 minutes before baking. Bake, uncovered, at 350° for 45-50 minutes or until a knife inserted near the center comes out clean. Let stand for 5 minutes before cutting.

TOMATO AND CHEESE STRATA

SAUSAGE-MUSHROOM BREAKFAST BAKE

SAUSAGE-MUSHROOM BREAKFAST BAKE
YIELD: 12 SERVINGS

My mom shared this delicious recipe when I needed to bring a dish to a breakfast potluck. Stuffed with savory sausage, flavorful mushrooms, cheese and egg, it was one breakfast casserole everyone raved about.

diane babbitt | ludlow, massachusetts

1	pound bulk pork sausage
2	cups sliced fresh mushrooms
6	cups cubed bread
2	cups (8 ounces) shredded sharp cheddar cheese
1	cup chopped fresh tomatoes
10	eggs, lightly beaten
3	cups milk
2	teaspoons ground mustard
1/2	teaspoon salt
1/4	teaspoon pepper

In a large skillet, cook sausage and mushrooms over medium heat until meat is no longer pink; drain. Place half of the bread cubes in a greased 13-in. x 9-in. baking dish; top with 2 cups sausage mixture and half of the cheese and tomatoes. Repeat layers. In a large bowl, combine the eggs, milk, mustard, salt and pepper; pour over bread mixture.

Bake, uncovered, at 350° for 50-55 minutes or until a knife inserted near the center comes out clean. Let stand for 10 minutes before serving.

PLEASING POTATO PIE
YIELD: 4-6 SERVINGS

Now that I'm retired, cooking has replaced teaching as my first love. I especially like to serve this hearty potato-and-egg dish for a relaxing morning meal with loved ones.

elizabeth leland | los alamos, new mexico

2	cups shredded peeled potatoes (about 1 pound)
1-1/2	cups (6 ounces) shredded cheddar cheese, *divided*
1	teaspoon salt, *divided*
4	eggs
1/2	cup milk
1	cup chopped fully cooked ham
1/2	cup chopped onion
1/2	teaspoon pepper

Combine the potatoes, 1/2 cup shredded cheddar cheese and 1/2 teaspoon salt. Press onto the bottom and up the sides of a greased 9-in. pie plate.

In a bowl, beat eggs and milk. Add ham, onion, pepper and remaining cheese and salt; pour over potato crust (dish will be very full). Bake at 350° for 45-50 minutes or until a knife inserted near the center comes out clean. Let stand for 5 minutes before cutting.

SWEET HAM STEAK
YIELD: 6-8 SERVINGS

You need just three ingredients to fix this sweetly seasoned ham slice. It's a quick and easy addition to any special occasion breakfast menu and a nice change of pace from traditional bacon or sausage side dishes.

nancy smits | markesan, wisconsin

1	bone-in fully cooked ham steak (2 pounds)
5	tablespoons butter, cubed
5	tablespoons brown sugar

In a large skillet over medium heat, brown ham steak on both sides; drain. Remove ham. In the same skillet, melt the butter; stir in brown sugar. Return ham to skillet; cook until heated through, turning often.

SWEET HAM STEAK

SAUSAGE BREAKFAST PIZZA

SAUSAGE BREAKFAST PIZZA
YIELD: 8 SERVINGS

Pizza for breakfast? You bet! Kids of all ages will love making and munching this hearty meal-in-one made with convenient crescent rolls and frozen hash browns. It's great for brunch or whenever you want to feed a lot of people at one time.

rae truax | mattawa, washington

1	tube (8 ounces) refrigerated crescent rolls
1	pound bulk pork sausage
1	cup frozen shredded hash brown potatoes, thawed
1	cup (4 ounces) shredded cheddar cheese
3	eggs
1/4	cup milk
1/4	teaspoon pepper
1/4	cup grated Parmesan cheese

Unroll crescent dough and place on a greased 12-in. pizza pan; press seams together and press up the sides of the pan to form a crust. In a large skillet, brown sausage over medium heat; drain and cool slightly. Sprinkle the sausage, hash browns and cheddar cheese over crust.

In a small bowl, whisk the eggs, milk and pepper; pour over pizza. Sprinkle egg mixture with Parmesan cheese. Bake at 375° for 28-30 minutes or until a knife inserted near the center comes out clean. Let the pizza stand 10 minutes before cutting into eight slices.

HOMEMADE PANCAKE SYRUP
YIELD: 1-1/2 CUPS

This simple maple syrup cooks up in minutes but leaves a lasting impression. It's best served hot over waffles, pancakes or French toast with lots of creamy butter.

jill hanns | klamath falls, oregon

3/4	cup packed brown sugar
1/4	cup sugar
3/4	cup water
1/2	cup light corn syrup
1/2	teaspoon maple flavoring
1/2	teaspoon vanilla extract

In a saucepan, combine the sugars, water and corn syrup; bring to a boil over medium heat. Boil for 7 minutes or until slightly thickened. Remove from the heat; stir in the maple flavoring and vanilla extract. Cool for 15 minutes. Serve over pancakes, waffles or French toast.

ZESTY CORN CAKES
YIELD: 4 SERVINGS

My family likes savory foods for breakfast instead of the typical "sweet" breads, like pancakes and French toast. In this recipe, golden corn cakes get a slight kick from the spicy, meaty filling. Both the cakes and filling pair wonderfully with the creamy cheese sauce.

catherine mc fann | premier, west virginia

1	pound ground beef
1	medium onion, chopped
1	small green pepper, chopped
1	celery rib, chopped
1	can (6 ounces) tomato paste
1/3	cup water
2	garlic cloves, minced
1	teaspoon chili powder
1	teaspoon salt
1/4	teaspoon pepper

CHEESE SAUCE:

8	ounces process American cheese, cubed
2/3	cup evaporated milk
1/2	teaspoon chili powder

CORN CAKES:

1	package (8-1/2 ounces) corn bread/muffin mix
1/2	cup evaporated milk
1/4	cup water
1	egg, beaten
2	tablespoons butter, melted

In a skillet, cook beef over medium heat until no longer pink; drain. Add the next nine ingredients; mix well. Bring to a boil. Reduce heat; simmer, uncovered for 2 minutes or until the mixture is thickened.

In a saucepan, combine the cheese sauce ingredients. Cook and stir over low heat until cheese is melted.

In a bowl, combine corn cake ingredients just until moistened. Pour 1/4 cupfuls of batter onto a hot greased griddle. Turn when bubbles form on top of cake. Cook until the second side is golden brown.

Place a corn cake on four serving plates. Top each with 1/4 cup of filling. Repeat layers once. Serve with cheese sauce.

CINNAMON RAISIN STRATA

CINNAMON RAISIN STRATA
YIELD: 4 SERVINGS

This delightful dish, made with day-old raisin bread, is full of comforting cinnamon flavor. I like to serve the baked specialty for brunch with sliced bacon and a fruit compote.

barbara tritch | hope, idaho

1/4	cup butter, softened
3	tablespoons ground cinnamon
8	slices day-old raisin bread
4	tablespoons brown sugar, *divided*
6	eggs
1-1/2	cups milk
3	tablespoons maple syrup
1	teaspoon vanilla extract

Additional maple syrup

In a small bowl, combine butter and cinnamon; spread over one side of each slice of bread. Place four slices, buttered side up, in a greased 8-in. square baking dish (trim to fit if necessary). Sprinkle with 2 tablespoons brown sugar. Repeat with remaining bread and brown sugar.

In a large bowl, whisk the eggs, milk, syrup and vanilla; pour over bread. Cover and refrigerate overnight. Remove from the refrigerator 30 minutes before baking. Bake, uncovered, at 350° for 40-50 minutes or until golden and puffed. Serve with additional syrup.

Breakfast TIP

The whisk you use to prepare eggs can be used to stir up muffins, waffles and pancakes, too. I've found that using a whisk mixes the batter more thoroughly and also combines it more quickly to prevent overmixing.

—Ro E., Buffalo, Wyoming

GOLDEN COUNTRY GRITS
YIELD: 8-10 SERVINGS

Although I was born and raised in the South, I never really cared for this truly Southern dish. But one day I was poring over my mother's collection of recipes, saw this and decided to give it a try. You might say I've been a fan of grits ever since.

sharon stovall | greenville, kentucky

4	cups cooked grits
1	cup (4 ounces) shredded sharp cheddar cheese
2	eggs, lightly beaten
1/4	cup butter
1	tablespoon minced fresh parsley
1/2	teaspoon salt

In a large bowl, combine all of the ingredients. Pour the grits mixture into a greased 1-1/2-qt. baking dish. Bake, uncovered, at 350° for 30 minutes or until golden brown.

BREAKFAST SAUSAGE PATTIES
YIELD: 4 SERVINGS

Ground turkey lightens up these pleasantly seasoned breakfast patties while cayenne gives them a slight kick. Serve them alongside scrambled eggs or pancakes.

carolyn sykora | bloomer, wisconsin

1	pound ground turkey
3/4	teaspoon salt
1/2	teaspoon rubbed sage
1/2	teaspoon dried thyme
1/2	teaspoon ground nutmeg
1/8	teaspoon cayenne pepper
2	teaspoons canola oil

In a large bowl, combine the turkey, salt, sage, thyme, nutmeg and cayenne. Shape into eight patties. In a large skillet, cook patties in oil over medium heat for 5 minutes on each side or until juices run clear. Drain on paper towels.

BREAKFAST SAUSAGE PATTIES

EYE-OPENING EGGS

RISE AND SHINE TO AN ASSORTMENT OF FARM-FRESH EGG DISHES THAT ARE SURE TO GIVE YOUR DAY A SUNNY START.

BACON VEGETABLE QUICHE
PAGE 22

Separating eggs doesn't have to be a messy chore and you don't need a fancy kitchen gadget. A simple, small funnel will do the trick. Just break the egg over the funnel. The egg white will run through the funnel, and the yolk will remain.

If you do happen to get a little bit of yolk in the egg whites, touch the yolk with a piece of bread. The yolk will adhere to the bread like magic.

MINI HAM 'N' CHEESE FRITTATAS

I found this recipe a few years ago and tried to make it with a few changes. Every time I serve a brunch, the frittatas are the first thing to disappear—and nobody knows they are low in fat!

susan watt | basking ridge, new jersey

MINI HAM 'N' CHEESE FRITTATAS
YIELD: 8 FRITTATAS

1/4	pound cubed fully cooked lean ham
1	cup (4 ounces) shredded fat-free cheddar cheese
6	eggs
4	egg whites
3	tablespoons minced chives
2	tablespoons fat-free milk
1/4	teaspoon salt
1/4	teaspoon pepper

Divide ham evenly among eight muffin cups coated with cooking spray; top with cheese. In a large bowl, beat eggs and whites. Beat in the chives, milk, salt and pepper. Pour over cheese, filling each muffin cup three-fourths full.

Bake at 375° for 22-25 minutes or until a knife inserted near the center comes out clean. Carefully run a knife around edges to loosen; remove from pan. Serve warm.

CHEESY O'BRIEN EGGS

This snappy breakfast bake is perfect for a brunch buffet or when out-of-town guests stay the night. Full of bacon, cheese and hash browns, the all-in-one egg dish is a hearty crowd-pleaser.

margaret edmondson | red oak, iowa

CHEESY O'BRIEN EGGS
YIELD: 12 SERVINGS

1	package (28 ounces) frozen O'Brien potatoes
1/2	teaspoon garlic salt
1/4	teaspoon pepper
1	can (10-3/4 ounces) condensed cheddar cheese soup, undiluted
1	pound sliced bacon, cooked and crumbled
12	eggs, lightly beaten
2	tablespoons butter
2	cups (8 ounces) shredded cheddar cheese

In a large skillet, prepare hash browns according to package directions. sprinkle with garlic salt and pepper. Transfer to a greased 2-1/2-qt. baking dish. Top with soup. Set aside 1/2 cup of bacon; sprinkle remaining bacon over soup.

In a bowl, whisk the eggs. In another large skillet, heat butter until hot. Add eggs; cook and stir over medium heat until eggs are nearly set. Spoon over bacon. Sprinkle with cheese and reserved bacon. Bake, uncovered, at 350° for 20-25 minutes or until cheese is melted.

TEX-MEX SCRAMBLE
YIELD: 2 SERVINGS

3	corn tortillas (6 inches), cut into thin strips
4	teaspoons olive oil, *divided*
2	tablespoons chopped onion
1	jalapeno pepper, seeded and chopped
4	eggs, lightly beaten
1	plum tomato, chopped
1/4	cup shredded cooked roast beef
1/8	teaspoon salt
1/8	teaspoon pepper
1/4	cup shredded Monterey Jack cheese

In a large nonstick skillet, cook tortilla strips in 2 teaspoons oil for 5 minutes or until lightly golden brown but not crisp. Add the onion, jalapeno and remaining oil; cook 2 minutes longer.

Add the eggs, tomato, beef, salt and pepper; cook and stir until eggs are completely set. Sprinkle with cheese; cover and let stand for 2-3 minutes until cheese is melted.

EDITOR'S NOTE: When cutting hot peppers, disposable gloves are recommended. Avoid touching your face.

TEX-MEX SCRAMBLE

This Southwestern mix of eggs, corn tortilla strips, roast beef and other savory ingredients is our favorite breakfast—and dinner—for two. Feel free to use a milder pepper if you don't care for a lot of spice.

paula wharton | el paso, texas

STRAWBERRY BANANA OMELET

STRAWBERRY BANANA OMELET
YIELD: 2-3 SERVINGS

Our home economists came up with an unusual filling for these quick and easy omelets. The sweet strawberry and banana combination makes for a dessert-like treat in the morning.

taste of home test kitchen

- 3 tablespoons butter, *divided*
- 2 tablespoons brown sugar
- 1/8 teaspoon ground cinnamon
- 2 medium firm bananas, sliced
- 1/4 teaspoon vanilla extract
- 1-1/2 cups sliced fresh strawberries
- 6 eggs
- 2 tablespoons water
- 1/2 teaspoon salt

In a small saucepan, heat 1 tablespoon butter, brown sugar and cinnamon over medium heat until sugar is dissolved. Add bananas and vanilla; toss to coat. Remove from the heat; stir in strawberries. Set aside.

In a large bowl, beat the eggs, water and salt. Heat remaining butter in a 10-in. nonstick skillet over medium heat; add the egg mixture. As the eggs set, lift edges, letting any uncooked portion flow underneath.

When eggs are almost set, spread two-thirds of fruit mixture over one side; fold omelet over filling. Cover and cook for 1-2 minutes or until heated through. Slide onto a serving plate; top with remaining fruit mixture.

Breakfast TIP

Leftover chili is great for omelets. Stuff the omelet with the reheated chili and top with lettuce, cheese, onions and sour cream.

—*Susan S., Twin Valley, Minnesota*

GARDEN BREAKFAST
YIELD: 2 SERVINGS

Healthy and simply delicious, this fluffy omelet is chock-full of garden-fresh veggies, reduced-fat cheese and flavor. It's a very versatile dish, too, allowing me to make it with whatever vegetables I happen to have on hand.

edie despain | logan, utah

- 4 egg whites
- 1/4 cup water
- 1/4 teaspoon cream of tartar
- 2 eggs
- 1/4 teaspoon salt
- 1 teaspoon butter
- 1 medium tomato, chopped
- 1 small zucchini, chopped
- 1 small onion, chopped
- 1/4 cup chopped green pepper
- 1/2 teaspoon Italian seasoning
- 1/3 cup shredded reduced-fat cheddar cheese

In a small bowl, beat the egg whites, water and cream of tartar until stiff peaks form. In a large bowl, beat eggs and salt until thick and lemon-colored, about 5 minutes. Fold in the egg whites.

Melt butter in a 10-in. nonstick ovenproof skillet coated with cooking spray. Add egg mixture. Cook over medium heat for 5 minutes or until puffed and lightly browned on the bottom. Bake, uncovered, at 350° for 10-12 minutes or until a knife inserted 2 in. from edge comes out clean.

Meanwhile, in a skillet, saute the tomato, zucchini, onion, green pepper and Italian seasoning until tender. Carefully run a knife around edge of omelet to loosen. With a sharp knife, score center of omelet. Place vegetables on one side and sprinkle with cheese; fold other side over filling. Slide onto a serving plate; cut in half.

GARDEN BREAKFAST

BACON VEGETABLE QUICHE

BACON VEGETABLE QUICHE
YIELD: 6 SERVINGS

This recipe is so versatile! You can use Vidalia onions, green onions or leeks. Asparagus can take the place of broccoli, and you can use whatever fresh herbs or cheese you have on hand. I especially like serving this savory egg bake in spring, when I am overwhelmed with an abundance of fresh produce.

shannon koene | *blacksburg, virginia*

1	unbaked pastry shell (9 inches)
2	cups fresh baby spinach
1	cup sliced fresh mushrooms
1	cup chopped fresh broccoli
3/4	cup chopped sweet onion
2-1/2	teaspoons olive oil
3	eggs, lightly beaten
1	can (5 ounces) evaporated milk
1	tablespoon minced fresh rosemary *or* 1 teaspoon dried rosemary, crushed
1/4	teaspoon salt
1/4	teaspoon pepper
1	cup (4 ounces) shredded cheddar cheese
6	bacon strips, cooked and crumbled
1/2	cup crumbled tomato and basil feta cheese

Line unpricked pastry shell with a double thickness of heavy-duty foil. Bake at 450° for 8 minutes. Remove foil; bake 5 minutes longer.

Meanwhile, in a large skillet, saute the spinach, mushrooms, broccoli and onion in oil until tender. In a large bowl, whisk the eggs, milk, rosemary, salt and pepper.

Using a slotted spoon, transfer vegetables to egg mixture. Stir in cheddar cheese and bacon. Pour into crust. Sprinkle with feta cheese.

Cover edges loosely with foil. Bake at 375° for 30-35 minutes or until a knife inserted near the center comes out clean. Let stand for 5 minutes before cutting.

SMOKED SAUSAGE SCRAMBLE
YIELD: 2 SERVINGS

I came up with this recipe one morning when we had smoked sausage leftover from the day before. The combination of spicy sausage, spinach, eggs, potato and cheese makes this scramble a perfect beginning to any day.

stephanie leven | *warsaw, missouri*

1	medium potato, cubed
1	tablespoon chopped onion
1	tablespoon canola oil
1	cup torn fresh spinach
1	cup cubed smoked sausage
4	eggs
1	tablespoon water
2	slices American cheese, diced

In a large skillet, cook potato and onion in oil until potato is tender; add spinach and sausage. In a large bowl, whisk eggs and water. Pour over sausage mixture. Cook and stir over medium heat, until eggs are completely set. Sprinkle eggs with diced cheese.

SMOKED SAUSAGE SCRAMBLE

CREAMED EGGS ON ENGLISH MUFFINS
YIELD: 4 SERVINGS

I came across this recipe when I first got married. Years later, it's still my husband's favorite for breakfast or brunch thanks to its rich and satisfying taste. Try it over plain toast, too.

barbara peterson | *indianapolis, indiana*

1/4	cup chopped onion
1	tablespoon butter
1/4	cup coarsely chopped fresh mushrooms
3/4	cup milk
1	package (8 ounces) cream cheese, softened

1/2 cup grated Parmesan cheese
2 tablespoons minced fresh parsley
1 teaspoon Dijon mustard
Salt and pepper to taste
6 hard-cooked eggs, coarsely chopped
4 English muffins, split and toasted

In a saucepan, saute onion in butter until almost tender. Add mushrooms; saute until mushrooms and onion are tender. Stir in milk and cream cheese; cook and stir until cheese is melted and blended. Stir in the Parmesan cheese, parsley, Dijon mustard, salt and pepper. Add the hard-cooked eggs; heat through. Serve egg mixture over toasted English muffins.

MEAT LOVER'S OMELET ROLL
YIELD: 8 SERVINGS

This hearty fare is fit for company. But when I do make it for just my husband and myself, we get to enjoy the luscious leftovers! The mustard sauce has just the right amount of bite and complements the fluffy omelet roll slices wonderfully.

roberta gibbs | kamiah, idaho

1 cup mayonnaise, *divided*
1 tablespoon prepared mustard
1-1/2 teaspoons prepared horseradish
1-1/2 teaspoons plus 1/4 cup finely chopped onion, *divided*
2 tablespoons all-purpose flour
12 eggs, *separated*
1 cup milk
1/2 teaspoon salt
1/8 teaspoon pepper
1/2 cup finely chopped celery
2 teaspoons canola oil
1 cup cubed fully cooked ham
3/4 cup cooked pork sausage, drained and crumbled
8 bacon strips, cooked and crumbled
1 cup (4 ounces) shredded Swiss cheese

For mustard sauce, in a small bowl, combine 1/2 cup mayonnaise, mustard, horseradish and 1-1/2 teaspoons onion until blended. Refrigerate until serving. Line a 15-in. x 10-in. x 1-in. baking pan with waxed paper; grease the paper and set aside.

In a large saucepan, combine flour and remaining mayonnaise until smooth. In a large bowl, whisk egg yolks until thickened. Add the milk, salt and pepper; whisk into flour mixture. Cook over medium-low heat for 6-7 minutes or until slightly thickened. Remove from the heat. Cool for 15 minutes.

In a large bowl, beat egg whites until stiff peaks form. Gradually fold into egg yolk mixture. Spread into prepared pan. Bake at 425° for 12-15 minutes or until golden brown.

Meanwhile, in a large skillet, saute celery and remaining onion in oil until crisp-tender. Add the ham, sausage and bacon; heat through and keep warm.

Remove omelet from oven. Run a knife around edges to loosen; invert onto a kitchen towel. Gently peel off waxed paper. Sprinkle cheese over omelet to within 1 in. of edges. Top with meat mixture. Roll up from a short side. Transfer to a serving platter, seam side down. Cut with a serrated knife. Serve with mustard sauce.

OVEN DENVER OMELET
YIELD: 6 SERVINGS

Fans of the classic Denver omelet will love this oven-baked take on a tried-and-true favorite. This casserole-like version packs in all the ingredients and flavor of the original, but is well suited for larger gatherings.

ellen bower | taneytown, maryland

8 eggs
1/2 cup half-and-half cream
1 cup (4 ounces) shredded cheddar cheese
1 cup finely chopped fully cooked ham
1/4 cup finely chopped green pepper
1/4 cup finely chopped onion

In a bowl, whisk eggs and cream. Stir in the cheese, ham, green pepper and onion. Pour into a greased 9-in. square baking dish. Bake at 400° for 25 minutes or until a knife inserted near the center comes out clean.

OVEN DENVER OMELET

ZUCCHINI FRITTATA

ZUCCHINI FRITTATA
YIELD: 6 SERVINGS

This frittata is so quick to make because it cooks in the microwave in just minutes! Plus, it's a great way to use extra zucchini from the garden. You can add a red pepper garnish for a colorful look.

mildred fox | fostoria, ohio

4	cups diced zucchini
1	small onion, chopped
4	eggs
1	cup (4 ounces) shredded cheddar cheese
1	cup cubed fully cooked ham
3/4	teaspoon salt
1/8	teaspoon pepper

In a 9-in. microwave-safe pie plate, combine the zucchini and onion. Cover and microwave on high for 3-4 minutes or until vegetables are tender; drain.

In a bowl, combine the eggs, cheese, ham, salt and pepper. Carefully pour over zucchini mixture. Microwave at 70% power for 8-9 minutes or until a knife inserted near the center comes out clean.

EDITOR'S NOTE: This recipe was tested in a 1,100-watt microwave.

NEST EGGS
YIELD: 6 SERVINGS

With just four ingredients, this No. 1 recipe is ready in about 30 minutes. The fun presentation and combination of egg and sausage are a hit with kids and adults.

jeannette westphal | gettysburg, south dakota

1	pound bulk pork sausage
6	hard-cooked eggs, shelled
1	envelope seasoned coating mix for chicken
1/4	cup milk

Divide the pork sausage into six equal portions. Pat each portion into a 4-1/2-in. x 3-in. rectangle and wrap around a hard-cooked egg, pressing to cover.

Place coating mix in a plastic bag. Dip egg in milk and shake in coating mix. Place eggs 1 in. apart on a baking sheet. Bake, uncovered, at 400° for 25-30 minutes or until lightly browned.

EGG 'N' POTATO BURRITOS
YIELD: 6 SERVINGS

This is my husband's choice way to enjoy eggs. The scrumptious combination of hash browns and scrambled eggs wrapped in soft flour tortillas adds zip to breakfasts on the fly.

ann yarber | washington, oklahoma

1	cup frozen shredded hash brown potatoes, thawed
3	green onions, chopped
1	tablespoon olive oil
8	eggs, lightly beaten
1	can (14-1/2 ounces) diced tomatoes with mild green chilies, drained
1/2	teaspoon salt
1/2	teaspoon pepper
6	fat-free flour tortillas (8 inches), warmed
1	cup (4 ounces) shredded reduced-fat cheddar cheese

In a large nonstick skillet, cook potatoes and onions in oil over medium heat for 8-10 minutes or until potatoes are tender, stirring occasionally.

In a large bowl, combine the eggs, tomatoes, salt and pepper. Pour over potatoes. Reduce heat to medium-low. Cook and stir until eggs are completely set. Remove from the heat.

Spoon about 1/2 cup of egg mixture down the center of each tortilla; sprinkle with cheddar cheese. Fold sides and ends of tortilla over filling and roll up.

EGG 'N' POTATO BURRITOS

CREAM CHEESE SCRAMBLED EGGS

My mother-in-law introduced me to this recipe, and now it's my kids' favorite choice for breakfast. The rich taste makes it special enough for holiday celebrations, but doesn't take up a lot of time on such a busy day.

jacque hunt | heyburn, idaho

CREAM CHEESE SCRAMBLED EGGS
YIELD: 4 SERVINGS

1	package (3 ounces) cream cheese, softened
2	tablespoons half-and-half cream
8	eggs
1/3	cup grated Parmesan cheese
1/2	teaspoon lemon-pepper seasoning
1/8	teaspoon salt
1/2	cup real bacon bits
2	tablespoons butter

In a small bowl, beat cream cheese and cream until smooth. Beat in the eggs, Parmesan cheese, lemon-pepper and salt. Stir in bacon. In a large skillet, melt butter; add egg mixture. Cook and stir over medium heat until eggs are completely set.

ASIAN OVEN OMELET
YIELD: 6 SERVINGS

2	packages (3 ounces *each*) ramen noodles
1/2	cup thinly sliced celery
2	teaspoons canola oil
1	package (8 ounces) sliced fresh mushrooms
4	tablespoons green onions, thinly sliced, *divided*
2	tablespoons minced fresh gingerroot
3	eggs
6	egg whites
1	teaspoon sesame oil
1/2	teaspoon sugar
1/2	teaspoon salt
2	tablespoons reduced-sodium soy sauce

Discard seasoning packet from ramen noodles or save for another use. Cook noodles according to package directions. Drain and rinse in cold water; transfer to a bowl and set aside.

Meanwhile, in a large nonstick ovenproof skillet over medium heat, cook celery in canola oil for 1 minute. Stir in the mushrooms, 2 tablespoons green onions and ginger; cook and stir for 7 minutes or until mushrooms are lightly browned. Stir into noodles.

Whisk the eggs, egg whites, sesame oil, sugar and salt. Stir egg mixture into noodle mixture; spread into an even layer in the skillet. Cook on medium for 2 minutes. Bake, uncovered at 350° for 10-12 minutes or until the eggs are completely set. Cut into wedges. Sprinkle with the remaining green onions. Drizzle with soy sauce.

ASIAN OVEN OMELET

If you enjoy egg foo yong, you're sure to like this recipe. It's a simple and inexpensive way to add healthy, lean protein to your diet.

edna hoffman | hebron, indiana

BACON 'N' EGG WRAPS

BACON 'N' EGG WRAPS
YIELD: 4 SERVINGS

The zip from salsa will wake up your taste buds when you bite into this hearty, handheld meal on-the-go. The burrito-like main dish makes a speedy and very filling breakfast.

sharonda baker | joliet, illinois

1	medium onion, chopped
3/4	cup chopped green pepper
1	tablespoon butter
5	eggs
1	tablespoon milk
1/2	teaspoon salt
1/4	teaspoon pepper
2	cups (8 ounces) shredded cheddar cheese
1/2	pound sliced bacon, cooked and crumbled
4	flour tortillas (10 inches), warmed

Salsa, optional

In a large nonstick skillet, saute onion and green pepper in butter until tender. In a large bowl, beat the eggs, milk, salt and pepper.

Pour over vegetables in the skillet. Sprinkle with cheese and bacon. Cook and stir gently over medium heat until the eggs are completely set.

Spoon 1/2 cup down the center of each tortilla; fold sides over filling. Serve with salsa if desired.

FARMER'S BREAKFAST
YIELD: 6 SERVINGS

I found this recipe in the newspaper several years ago and loved it. It was especially handy when I needed something to serve overnight guests because I can whip it up in no time flat.

lynn ames | idaho falls, idaho

3	cups finely chopped peeled potatoes (about 3 medium)
1/4	cup chopped green pepper
3	tablespoons butter
9	eggs
3	tablespoons milk
1/4	teaspoon pepper
1-1/2	cups cubed fully cooked ham
1	jar (4-1/2 ounces) sliced mushrooms, drained
1/4	cup shredded cheddar cheese

In a 2-qt. microwave-safe dish, combine the potatoes, green pepper and butter. Cover and microwave on high for 7-8 minutes or until vegetables are tender, stirring once.

In a large bowl, beat the eggs, milk and pepper; stir in ham and mushrooms. Stir into potato mixture. Cover and microwave at 70% power for 8-10 minutes or until eggs are almost set, stirring every 2 minutes.

Sprinkle with cheese. Cook, uncovered, on high for 1-2 minutes or until cheese is melted and eggs are completely set.

EDITOR'S NOTE: This recipe was tested in a 1,100-watt microwave.

FARMER'S BREAKFAST

CHICKEN SPINACH QUICHE
YIELD: 6-8 SERVINGS

This deliciously different quiche features diced chicken, healthy spinach and flavorful cheddar cheese, making it a satisfying choice for both brunch and dinner. I sometimes substitute Swiss cheese for cheddar with equally tasty results.

barbara mccalley | allison park, pennsylvania

1	cup (4 ounces) shredded cheddar cheese, *divided*
1	unbaked pastry shell (9 inches)
1	cup diced cooked chicken
1	package (10 ounces) frozen chopped spinach, thawed and squeezed dry
1/4	cup finely chopped onion
2	eggs
3/4	cup milk
3/4	cup mayonnaise
1/4	teaspoon salt
1/8	teaspoon pepper

Sprinkle 1/4 cup cheese into the pastry shell. In a bowl, combine the chicken, 1/2 cup spinach, onion and remaining cheese (save remaining spinach for another use). Spoon into pastry shell. In a bowl, whisk the eggs, milk, mayonnaise, salt and pepper; pour over the chicken mixture.

Bake at 350° for 40-45 minutes or until a knife inserted near the center comes out clean. Let the quiche stand for 15 minutes before cutting.

EDITOR'S NOTE: Reduced-fat or fat-free mayonnaise is not recommended for this recipe.

HEARTY SCRAMBLED EGGS
YIELD: 4 SERVINGS

This yummy scramble includes classic omelet ingredients in a fun skillet dish that's so quick to make! The eggs pick up plenty of flavor from the mushrooms, onion and cheese. To shave minutes off the prep time, I keep diced ham on hand in the freezer.

carole anhalt | manitowoc, wisconsin

8	eggs
1-1/4	cups diced fully cooked ham
3/4	cup diced cheddar cheese
1/2	cup chopped fresh mushrooms
1/4	cup chopped onion
2	to 3 tablespoons butter

In a bowl, beat eggs. Add ham, cheese, mushrooms and onion. Melt butter in a skillet; add egg mixture. Cook and stir over medium heat until eggs are completely set and cheese is melted.

HEARTY SCRAMBLED EGGS

Breakfast TIP

SWISS OMELET ROLL-UP
YIELD: 10-12 SERVINGS

My family enjoys this scrumptious and unique omelet on Christmas morning after we've opened gifts. However, I've found it's wonderful morning fare for any time of year. Its special taste and appearance make the preparation time worthwhile.

gertrude dumas | athol, massachusetts

1-1/2	cups mayonnaise, *divided*
2	tablespoons all-purpose flour
12	eggs, *separated*
1	cup milk
1/2	teaspoon salt
1/8	teaspoon pepper
6	tablespoons chopped green onions, *divided*
1	tablespoon Dijon mustard
1-1/2	cups chopped fully cooked ham
1	cup (4 ounces) shredded Swiss cheese

Fresh oregano *or* parsley, optional

In a saucepan, combine 1/2 cup mayonnaise and flour. In a bowl, whisk egg yolks until thickened; add milk. Pour into mayonnaise mixture; cook over low heat, stirring constantly, until thickened. Add salt and pepper. Remove from the heat; cool for 15 minutes.

In a bowl, beat egg whites until stiff. Fold into the mayonnaise mixture. Line a 15-in. x 10-in. x 1-in. baking pan with waxed paper; coat paper with cooking spray. Pour egg mixture into pan. Bake at 425° for 20 minutes.

Meanwhile, in a saucepan over low heat, combine 2 tablespoon onions, mustard and remaining mayonnaise. Set aside 3/4 cup for topping; set aside and keep warm. To the remaining sauce, add ham, cheese and remaining onions; cook over low heat until cheese begins to melt.

Remove omelet from oven; turn onto a linen towel. Peel off waxed paper. Spread cheese sauce over warm omelet. Roll up from a short side. Top with reserved mustard sauce. Garnish with oregano or parsley if desired. Serve immediately.

EDITOR'S NOTE: Reduced-fat or fat-free mayonnaise is not recommended for this recipe.

CHEDDAR SALMON QUICHE
YIELD: 6 SERVINGS

My mother-in-law shared the recipe for this elegant morning dish. It dresses up convenient canned salmon in a very satisfying way. We enjoy this pretty quiche frequently and never tire of it.

jane horn | bellevue, ohio

1	cup all-purpose flour
1/4	teaspoon salt
3	tablespoons cold butter
3	tablespoons shortening
1/4	cup milk

FILLING:

1	can (14-3/4 ounces) salmon, drained, bones and skin removed
1	cup (4 ounces) shredded cheddar cheese
1/4	cup chopped green pepper
1/4	cup chopped onion
1	tablespoon all-purpose flour
1/2	teaspoon salt
1/8	teaspoon pepper
3	eggs
1-1/4	cups milk

In a large bowl, combine the flour and salt; cut in butter and shortening until crumbly. Stir in milk.

On a floured surface, roll dough into a 10-in. circle. Transfer to an ungreased 9-in. pie plate or quiche dish. Trim and flute edges. Bake at 350° for 10 minutes.

In a large bowl, combine salmon, cheese, green pepper, onion, flour, salt and pepper; spoon into crust. Combine the eggs and milk; pour over salmon mixture.

Bake for 50-55 minutes or until a knife inserted near the center comes out clean. Let quiche stand for 10 minutes before cutting into wedges.

CHEDDAR SALMON QUICHE

MINI SPINACH FRITTATAS

MINI SPINACH FRITTATAS
YIELD: 2 DOZEN

These mini frittatas are a cinch to make and absolutely delicious. The recipe doubles easily for a crowd and freezes well.

nancy statkevicus | tucson, arizona

1	cup ricotta cheese
3/4	cup grated Parmesan cheese
2/3	cup chopped fresh mushrooms
1	package (10 ounces) frozen chopped spinach, thawed and squeezed dry
1	egg
1/2	teaspoon dried oregano
1/4	teaspoon salt
1/4	teaspoon pepper
24	slices pepperoni

In a small bowl, combine the first eight ingredients. Place a slice of pepperoni in each of 24 greased miniature muffin cups. Fill muffin cups three-fourths full with cheese mixture.

Bake at 375° for 20-25 minutes or until a toothpick comes out clean. Carefully run a knife around edges of muffin cups to loosen. Serve warm.

SOUTHWESTERN EGGS
YIELD: 6-8 SERVINGS

Cooking is a hobby I've enjoyed for as long as I can remember. I love experimenting with new recipes and trying them out on my willing family of taste-testers. This was one such "experiment" that received rave-winning results from my test panel.

shirley seitz | affton, missouri

1	pound bulk pork sausage
1	medium onion, chopped

1/2 pound sliced fresh mushrooms
1/4 teaspoon salt
1/4 teaspoon pepper
6 eggs
3 tablespoons milk *or* heavy whipping cream
1 can (10 ounces) diced tomatoes with green chilies, drained
1/2 cup *each* shredded cheddar, part-skim mozzarella and Monterey Jack cheeses

In a large skillet, cook the sausage, onion, mushrooms, salt and pepper over medium heat until meat is no longer pink; drain and set aside.

In a blender, process the eggs and milk for 1 minute or until smooth. Pour into a greased shallow 1-1/2-qt. baking dish; bake at 400° for 5 minutes. Cover with the diced tomatoes with green chilies and the sausage mixture. Sprinkle with cheddar, mozzarella and Monterey Jack cheeses. Reduce heat to 350°; bake 20 minutes longer or until heated through.

MONTEREY TURKEY OMELET

MONTEREY TURKEY OMELET
YIELD: 2-3 SERVINGS

Our home economists use deli turkey, onion, garlic and green pepper to give a tasteful twist to a sunrise staple. The cheese-topped omelet looks special enough for company but leaves brunch hosts with plenty of time to relax with guests.

taste of home test kitchen

4 ounces thinly sliced deli smoked turkey, chopped
1/3 cup chopped onion
1/4 cup diced green pepper
1/2 teaspoon minced garlic
3 tablespoons butter, *divided*
6 eggs
3 tablespoons water
1/2 cup shredded Monterey Jack cheese

In a large skillet, cook the turkey, onion, green pepper and garlic in 2 tablespoons butter until the vegetables are tender. Remove and keep warm. In the same skillet, melt the remaining butter.

In a bowl, beat the eggs and water. Pour into skillet; cook over medium heat. As eggs set, lift the edges, letting uncooked portion flow underneath. When eggs are nearly set, spoon turkey mixture over half of the omelet. Fold omelet over filling. Sprinkle with cheese. Cover and let stand for 1-2 minutes or until cheese is melted.

DILLY SCRAMBLED EGGS
YIELD: 4 SERVINGS

With fresh dill flavor and a sprinkling of cheese, these scrambled eggs pack in plenty of farm-fresh flavor and cook in minutes for a speedy, flavorful and nutritious start to your day.

edna hoffman | hebron, indiana

6 eggs
1/4 cup water
1/2 teaspoon salt
Dash pepper
2 tablespoons butter
1/4 cup shredded cheddar cheese
1 teaspoon snipped fresh dill *or* 1/4 teaspoon dill weed

In a bowl, beat the eggs, water, salt and pepper. Melt butter in a skillet; add egg mixture. Cook and stir gently over medium heat until eggs are almost set. Sprinkle with cheddar cheese and dill. Cook until the eggs are completely set and the cheese is melted.

DILLY SCRAMBLED EGGS

PANCAKES & CREPES

TOPPED WITH FRESH FRUIT OR DRENCHED IN A BUTTERY SYRUP, THESE GOLDEN TEMPTATIONS ARE SURE TO PLEASE.

PUFFY OVEN PANCAKES
PAGE 40

The quintessential breakfast food, pancakes allow a lot of room for cooking creativity. The next time you whip up a batch, try these tasty suggestions:

- *When mixing the batter, add a dash of maple syrup.*
- *Beat in a bit of vanilla and cinnamon along with the eggs.*
- *In place of butter, spread peanut butter on a stack of pancakes.*
- *Replace milk with apple cider for great apple flavor in every bite.*

BLUEBERRY SOUR CREAM PANCAKES

Serve these light pancakes as is with blueberries inside and out. Or prepare them as simple, classic pancakes without the blueberries and serve with butter and warm maple syrup.

paula hadley | somerville, louisiana

BLUEBERRY SOUR CREAM PANCAKES
YIELD: ABOUT 20 PANCAKES (3-1/2 CUPS TOPPING)

1/2	cup sugar
2	tablespoons cornstarch
1	cup cold water
4	cups fresh *or* frozen blueberries

PANCAKES:

2	cups all-purpose flour
1/4	cup sugar
4	teaspoons baking powder
1/2	teaspoon salt
2	eggs
1-1/2	cups milk
1	cup (8 ounces) sour cream
1/3	cup butter, melted
1	cup fresh *or* frozen blueberries

In a large saucepan, combine the sugar and cornstarch. Stir in water until smooth. Add blueberries. Bring to a boil over medium heat; cook and stir for 2 minutes or until thickened. Remove from the heat; cover and keep warm.

For pancakes, in a large bowl, combine the flour, sugar, baking powder and salt. Combine the eggs, milk, sour cream and butter. Stir into dry ingredients just until moistened. Fold in the blueberries.

Pour batter by 1/4 cupful onto a greased hot griddle. Turn when bubbles form on top; cook until the second side is golden brown. Serve with blueberry topping.

EDITOR'S NOTE: If using frozen blueberries, don't thaw before adding to batter.

BROCCOLI CHEESE CREPES

BROCCOLI CHEESE CREPES
YIELD: 6 FILLED CREPES

Stuffed with a cheesy broccoli mixture, these crepes are perfect for a special brunch or light dinner for two. They are surprisingly easy to prepare and go wonderfully with the rich filling.

jane shapton | tustin, california

2	eggs
1/4	cup water
6	tablespoons all-purpose flour
1/2	teaspoon salt

FILLING:
2	tablespoons chopped onion
1	tablespoon butter
1	tablespoon all-purpose flour
1	cup milk
1	cup (4 ounces) shredded cheddar cheese, *divided*
1	to 1-1/2 teaspoons Dijon mustard
1	teaspoon Worcestershire sauce
1/4	teaspoon pepper
1/8	teaspoon salt
2	cups frozen chopped broccoli, thawed

For batter, combine the eggs, water, flour and salt in a blender. Cover and process until smooth; let stand for 15 minutes.

Meanwhile, for filling, in a small saucepan, saute onion in butter until tender. Stir in flour until blended. Gradually stir in milk. Bring to a boil over medium heat, stirring constantly; cook and stir for 2 minutes or until slightly thickened. Reduce heat to low. Stir in 1/2 cup cheese, mustard, Worcestershire sauce, pepper and salt. Stir until cheese is melted. Stir in broccoli. Cover; keep warm.

Heat a lightly greased 8-in. nonstick skillet; pour 2 tablespoons batter into the center of skillet. Lift and tilt pan to evenly coat bottom. Cook until top appears dry; turn and cook 15-20 seconds longer. Remove to a wire rack. Repeat with remaining batter, greasing skillet as needed.

Spoon about 1/2 cup filling down the center of each crepe; roll up. Place seam side down in an ungreased 11-in. x 7-in. baking dish. Sprinkle with remaining cheese. Bake, uncovered, at 350° for 5-7 minutes or until cheese is melted.

BIG APPETITE PANCAKES
YIELD: 85 SERVINGS

My church uses this recipe for its annual pancake and sausage breakfast with great success. At the breakfast, we also serve homemade sweet rolls, scrambled eggs, fruit, coffee and milk.

annabell seidl | ruth, michigan

12	eggs
3	quarts milk
12	cups all-purpose flour
3/4	cup sugar
3/4	cup baking powder
2	tablespoons salt
1-1/2	cups canola oil

Beat eggs; add milk. Add the dry ingredients and oil; mix well. Spoon the batter onto hot greased griddles. Turn when bubbles form on top. Cook until second side is golden brown.

CREAMY RHUBARB CREPES
YIELD: 10 CREPES

Fixing rhubarb this way brings a spring "zing" to the table. I adapted this crepe recipe, which originally featured strawberry jelly as the filling, from one I loved as a child. My husband declared it a "winner." He even came up with the recipe's name.

stasha wampler | gate city, virginia

3	eggs
1	cup milk
5	tablespoons butter, melted
1/4	cup sugar
1/4	teaspoon salt
1	cup all-purpose flour

Additional butter
SAUCE/FILLING:
1	cup sugar
1	tablespoon cornstarch
1/4	teaspoon ground cinnamon
2	cups thinly sliced fresh *or* frozen rhubarb, thawed
1	package (8 ounces) cream cheese, softened

Confectioners' sugar

In a large bowl, whisk eggs, milk, melted butter, sugar and salt. Beat in flour until smooth; let stand for 30 minutes.

Melt 1/2 teaspoon butter in an 8-in. nonstick skillet. Pour 1/4 cup batter into the center of skillet; lift and turn pan to cover bottom. Cook until lightly browned; turn and brown the other side. Remove to a wire rack; cover with paper towel. Repeat with remaining batter, adding butter to skillet as needed.

Meanwhile, for sauce, combine the sugar, cornstarch and cinnamon in a saucepan. Stir in rhubarb. Bring to a boil over medium heat; cook and stir for 2 minutes or until slightly thickened and the rhubarb is tender. Remove sauce from the heat; cool slightly.

For filling, in a bowl, beat cream cheese and 1/4 cup of the rhubarb sauce until smooth and creamy. Place a rounded tablespoonful on each crepe; fold in half and in half again, forming a triangle. Dust with confectioners' sugar. Serve the crepes with remaining sauce.

EDITOR'S NOTE: If using frozen rhubarb, measure rhubarb while still frozen, then thaw completely. Drain in a colander, but do not press liquid out.

CREAMY RHUBARB CREPES

BUTTERMILK PANCAKES
YIELD: 2-1/2 DOZEN

You just can't beat a basic buttermilk pancake for a down-home, hearty breakfast. Pair the fluffy flapjacks with sausage and fresh fruit for a mouth-watering morning meal.

betty abrey | imperial, saskatchewan

- 4 cups all-purpose flour
- 1/4 cup sugar
- 2 teaspoons baking soda
- 2 teaspoons salt
- 1-1/2 teaspoons baking powder
- 4 eggs
- 4 cups buttermilk

In a large bowl, combine the flour, sugar, baking soda, salt and baking powder. In another bowl, whisk the eggs and buttermilk until blended; stir the egg mixture into dry ingredients just until moistened.

Pour batter by 1/4 cupfuls onto a lightly greased hot griddle; turn when bubbles form on top. Cook until second side is golden brown.

BRAN GRIDDLE CAKES
YIELD: 14 PANCAKES

You'd never guess there's bran in these moist, tasty hotcakes that are drizzled with a sweet orange sauce. My children are grown, but they still request this for breakfast when they come home. Your family will surely flip over them, too!

marie cockerham | rock hill, south carolina

- 1-1/2 cups all-purpose flour
- 2 tablespoons sugar
- 3 teaspoons baking powder
- 3/4 teaspoon salt
- 1 egg
- 2 cups fat-free milk
- 1 teaspoon grated orange peel
- 1 cup All-Bran

ORANGE SYRUP:
- 1/2 cup sugar
- 1 tablespoon cornstarch
- 1 cup orange juice
- 1 tablespoon butter
- 2 teaspoons grated orange peel
- 1 medium navel orange, peeled, sectioned and chopped

In a bowl, combine the flour, sugar, baking powder and salt. In another bowl, beat egg; stir in milk, orange peel and bran cereal. Let stand for 1-2 minutes or until cereal is softened. Add to the dry ingredients; mix well.

Pour batter by 1/4 cupfuls onto a hot nonstick griddle; turn when bubbles form on top of pancakes. Cook until second side is golden brown.

For syrup, combine the sugar and cornstarch in a saucepan. Gradually stir in the orange juice, butter and orange peel. Bring to a boil; cook and stir for 2 minutes or until thickened. Remove the syrup from the heat; stir in the chopped orange. Serve the orange syrup with pancakes.

BRAN GRIDDLE CAKES

MULTIGRAIN PANCAKES

MULTIGRAIN PANCAKES
YIELD: 8 PANCAKES

My husband and I love foods prepared with whole grains, but our children do not. To satisfy everyone, I created this recipe to appeal to their love of pancakes while giving them a taste of whole grain cooking. It was a success!

ann harris | lancaster, california

1/2   cup all-purpose flour
1/4   cup whole wheat flour
1/4   cup cornmeal
2   tablespoons sugar
1/2   teaspoon baking soda
1/2   teaspoon salt
1   egg
1   cup buttermilk
2   tablespoons butter, melted
Maple syrup

In a large bowl, combine the first six ingredients. In a small bowl, whisk the egg, buttermilk and butter. Stir into dry ingredients just until moistened.

Pour batter by 1/4 cupfuls onto a greased hot griddle; turn when bubbles form on top. Cook until the second side is golden brown. Serve with syrup.

ZUCCHINI CREPES
YIELD: 12 CREPES

By keeping a few of these tender stuffed crepes in the freezer, I can easily reheat them when time is running short. Plus, they're a great way to use up extra zucchini.

patricia moyer | island pond, vermont

1   cup all-purpose flour
2   eggs

1/2   cup egg substitute
1-1/2   cups fat-free milk
3/4   teaspoon salt
FILLING:
1   large onion, chopped
1   medium green pepper, chopped
1   cup sliced fresh mushrooms
1   tablespoon canola oil
1   medium zucchini, shredded and squeezed dry
2   medium tomatoes, chopped and seeded
1-1/2   cups (6 ounces) shredded reduced-fat cheddar cheese, *divided*
1/4   teaspoon salt
1/4   teaspoon dried oregano
1/8   teaspoon pepper
1-1/2   cups meatless spaghetti sauce

In a large bowl, whisk together the flour, eggs, egg substitute, milk and salt until smooth. Cover and refrigerate for 1 hour.

Heat an 8-in. nonstick skillet coated with cooking spray; pour about 1/4 cup batter into center of skillet. Lift and tilt pan to evenly coat bottom. Cook until top appears dry; turn and cook 15-20 seconds longer. Remove to a wire rack. Repeat with remaining batter, coat with cooking spray as needed. When crepes are cool, stack crepes with waxed paper or paper towels in between.

For filling, in a large skillet, saute the onion, green pepper and mushrooms in oil until tender. Add the zucchini; saute 2-3 minutes longer. Remove from the heat; stir in tomatoes, 1 cup of cheese, salt, oregano and pepper.

Spoon vegetable mixture onto crepes and roll up. Arrange in a 13-in. x 9-in. baking dish coated with cooking spray. Spread spaghetti sauce over the crepes.

Cover and bake at 350° for 15-20 minutes. Sprinkle with remaining cheese. Bake, uncovered, 5 minutes longer or until the cheese is melted.

ZUCCHINI CREPES

APPLE RAISIN CREPES
YIELD: 1 DOZEN

1-1/2	cups all-purpose flour
1/4	cup sugar
1	cup milk
6	tablespoons water
1/4	cup canola oil
1	egg

FILLING:

5	cups thinly sliced peeled tart apples
1	cup sugar
1/2	cup raisins
2	teaspoons ground cinnamon
1	tablespoon confectioners' sugar

For batter, in a small bowl, combine flour and sugar. Add the milk, water, oil and egg. Cover and refrigerate for 1 hour.

For filling, in a large saucepan, combine the apples, sugar, raisins and cinnamon. Cook and stir over medium heat for 8-10 minutes or until apples are tender; set aside.

Heat a lightly greased 8-in. nonstick skillet; pour 3 tablespoons of batter into the center of skillet. Lift and tilt pan to evenly coat bottom. Cook until top appears dry; turn and cook 15-20 seconds longer. Remove to a wire rack. Repeat with remaining batter, greasing skillet as needed. When cool, stack crepes with waxed paper or paper towels in between.

With a slotted spoon, fill each crepe with 1/4 cup of apples; roll up. On a lightly greased griddle or in a large skillet, cook crepes over medium heat for 3-4 minutes on each side or until golden brown. Sprinkle crepes with confectioners' sugar. Serve immediately with remaining sauce.

APPLE RAISIN CREPES

I've been making and eating these delectable breakfast treats for as long as I can remember. They look impressive but are quick and easy to prepare. Heating the filled crepes a second time turns them golden brown and adds a wonderful crispness.

darlene brenden | salem, oregon

CINNAMON PANCAKES
YIELD: 12 PANCAKES

2	cups whole wheat flour
4	teaspoons baking powder
1	teaspoon ground cinnamon
1/2	teaspoon salt
2	eggs, lightly beaten
2	cups fat-free milk
2	tablespoons honey
1	tablespoon canola oil
1	medium apple, chopped

In a large bowl, combine the flour, baking powder, cinnamon and salt. Combine the eggs, milk, honey and oil; stir into dry ingredients just until moistened. Stir in apple.

Pour batter by 1/3 cupfuls onto a hot griddle coated with cooking spray. Turn when bubbles form on top; cook until second side is golden brown.

CINNAMON PANCAKES

My family adores the classic flavor combination of cinnamon and apples in these light yet hearty pancakes.

kim mcconnell | tulsa, oklahoma

SWEDISH PANCAKES

SWEDISH PANCAKES
YIELD: 20 PANCAKES

When we spend the night at my mother-in-law's house, our kids beg for these crepe-like pancakes for breakfast. They're a little lighter than traditional pancakes, so my family always eats a lot!

susan johnson | lyons, kansas

2	cups milk
4	eggs
1	tablespoon canola oil
1-1/2	cups all-purpose flour
3	tablespoons sugar
1/4	teaspoon salt

Lingonberries *or* raspberries
Seedless raspberry jam *or* fruit spread, warmed
Whipped topping

In a blender, combine the first six ingredients. Cover and process until blended. Heat a lightly greased 8-in. nonstick skillet; pour 1/4 cup batter into center of skillet. Lift and tilt pan to evenly coat bottom. Cook until top appears dry; turn and cook 15-20 seconds longer.

Repeat with remaining batter, adding oil to skillet as needed. Stack pancakes with waxed paper or paper towels in between. Reheat in the microwave if desired.

Fold pancakes into quarters; serve with berries, raspberry jam and whipped topping.

FRUIT-TOPPED BLINTZES
YIELD: 6-8 SERVINGS

My mother is a wonderful cook who likes to prepare (and improve on) dishes she samples at various restaurants. I followed her lead and did the same with these blintzes. My family loves my berry version even more than the original.

patricia larsen | thayne, wyoming

BLINTZES:

9	eggs
1	cup all-purpose flour
1/4	cup cornstarch
1/8	teaspoon salt
3	cups milk

FILLING:

2	packages (8 ounces *each*) cream cheese, softened
1/2	cup confectioners' sugar

Pureed raspberries *or* strawberries
Whipped cream, optional
Fresh raspberries *or* strawberries, optional

In a large bowl, beat eggs. Add flour, cornstarch and salt; stir until smooth. Stir in milk.

Heat a lightly greased 8-in. nonstick skillet; pour 1/3 cup batter into the center of skillet. Lift and tilt pan to evenly coat bottom. Cook until top appears dry; turn and cook 15-20 seconds longer. Keep in a warm oven, covered with foil. Repeat with remaining batter.

For filling, in a small bowl, beat cream cheese and confectioners' sugar until smooth. Place about 2 tablespoons in the center of each blintz; overlap sides and ends on top of filling. Place folded side down. Top with pureed berries; garnish with whipped cream and fresh berries if desired.

RASPBERRY KEY LIME CREPES
YIELD: 6 CREPES

Key lime juice turns cream cheese into a refreshing filling for these tender crepes. Sometimes, I even pipe the sweet filling into phyllo-dough cones that I bake separately.

wolfgang hanau | west palm beach, florida

RASPBERRY KEY LIME CREPES

1	package (12.3 ounces) silken firm tofu, crumbled
6	ounces reduced-fat cream cheese, cubed
2/3	cup confectioners' sugar, *divided*
2-1/2	teaspoons grated lime peel

Dash salt

Dash ground nutmeg

6	prepared crepes (9 inches)
1-1/2	cups fresh raspberries

In a blender, combine the lime juice, tofu and cream cheese; cover and process until smooth. Set aside 1 teaspoon confectioners' sugar. Add the lime peel, salt, nutmeg and remaining confectioners' sugar; cover and process until blended. Cover and refrigerate for at least 1 hour.

Spread cream cheese mixture over crepes. Sprinkle with raspberries; roll up. Dust with reserved confectioners' sugar.

SUNRISE ORANGE PANCAKES

SUNRISE ORANGE PANCAKES
YIELD: 12 PANCAKES

These delectable, citrusy pancakes make any morning special. You'll love how easily they come together.

dorothy smith | el dorado, arkansas

7	tablespoons sugar, *divided*
1-1/2	teaspoons cornstarch
1-1/2	cups orange juice, *divided*
2	cups biscuit/baking mix
2	eggs
3/4	cup milk

In a saucepan, combine 4 tablespoons sugar, cornstarch and 3/4 cup orange juice; stir until smooth. Bring to a boil; cook and stir for 2 minutes. Remove from heat; cool to lukewarm.

Meanwhile, combine biscuit mix and remaining sugar in a bowl. Beat the eggs, milk and remaining orange juice; stir into

dry ingredients just until moistened. Pour the batter by 1/4 cupfuls onto a lightly greased hot griddle; turn when bubbles form on top of pancakes. Cook until second side is golden brown. Serve with the orange sauce.

YOGURT PANCAKES
YIELD: 12 PANCAKES

Get your day off to a great start with these delicious yogurt pancakes. Whip up a quick batch on the weekend—varying the fillings—and pop them in your freezer. Then, savor these light, fluffy flapjacks throughout the week.

cheryll baber | homedale, idaho

2	cups all-purpose flour
2	tablespoons sugar
2	teaspoons baking powder
1	teaspoon baking soda
2	eggs
2	cups (16 ounces) plain yogurt
1/4	cup water

Semisweet chocolate chips, dried cranberries, sliced ripe bananas and coarsely chopped pecans, optional

In a small bowl, combine the flour, sugar, baking powder and baking soda. In another bowl, whisk the eggs, yogurt and water. Stir into dry ingredients just until moistened.

Pour batter by 1/4 cupfuls onto a hot griddle coated with cooking spray. Sprinkle with chocolate chips, cranberries, bananas or pecans if desired. Turn when bubbles form on top; cook until the second side is golden brown. Serve with bananas or pecans if desired.

To freeze, arrange cooled pancakes in a single layer on sheet pans. Freeze overnight or until frozen. Transfer to a resealable plastic freezer bag. May be frozen for up to 2 months.

To use frozen pancakes: Place pancake on a microwave-safe plate; microwave the pancakes on high for 40-50 seconds or until heated through.

YOGURT PANCAKES

HIGH-OCTANE PANCAKES

HIGH-OCTANE PANCAKES
YIELD: 4 PANCAKES

Fluffy and health-packed, these hotcakes are what I rely on to jump-start frosty winter mornings. The nutritious breakfast keeps me fueled for hours. They're scrumptious!

kelly hanlon | strasburg, colorado

1/3	cup plus 1 tablespoon all-purpose flour
1/4	cup quick-cooking oats
3	tablespoons toasted wheat germ
2	teaspoons sugar
1-1/4	teaspoons baking powder
1/8	teaspoon salt
2/3	cup fat-free milk
1/4	cup fat-free plain yogurt
1	tablespoon canola oil

In a small bowl, combine the first six ingredients. In another bowl, combine the milk, yogurt and oil. Stir into dry ingredients just until moistened.

Pour batter by 1/3 cupfuls onto a hot nonstick griddle coated with cooking spray. Turn when bubbles form on top of pancake; cook until second side is golden brown.

BLINTZ PANCAKES
YIELD: 12 PANCAKES

Blending sour cream and cottage cheese—ingredients traditionally associated with blintzes—into the batter of these pancakes provides them with their old-fashioned flavor. Top the family favorites with berry syrup to make an ordinary meal extraordinary.

dianna digoy | san diego, california

1	cup all-purpose flour
1	tablespoon sugar
1/2	teaspoon salt
1	cup (8 ounces) sour cream
1	cup (8 ounces) 4% cottage cheese

4	eggs, lightly beaten

Strawberry *or* blueberry syrup
Sliced fresh strawberries, optional

In a large bowl, combine the flour, sugar and salt. Stir in the sour cream, cottage cheese and eggs until blended.

Pour batter by 1/4 cupful onto a greased hot griddle in batches; turn when bubbles form on top. Cook until the second side is golden brown. Serve pancakes with syrup and strawberries if desired.

CORNMEAL PANCAKES
YIELD: 4 SERVINGS

I like to joke that these pancakes are so light, you have to hold them down! When we have a chance, we'll make them with freshly ground cornmeal bought at local festivals.

betty claycomb | alverton, pennsylvania

1-1/3	cups all-purpose flour
2/3	cup cornmeal
2	tablespoons sugar
4	teaspoons baking powder
1	teaspoon salt
2	eggs
1-1/3	cups milk
1/4	cup canola oil

Pancake syrup

In a large bowl, combine the flour, cornmeal, sugar, baking powder and salt. In another bowl, whisk the eggs, milk and oil; stir into dry ingredients just until moistened.

Pour batter by 1/4 cupfuls onto a lightly greased hot griddle. Turn when bubbles form on top; cook until the second side is golden brown. Serve with syrup.

CORNMEAL PANCAKES

CREAMY BANANA CREPES

YIELD: 1 DOZEN

My husband and I enjoy taking turns fixing weekend breakfasts. These crepes are frequently on our menus. The sweet-and-sour banana filling is delicious. You'll want to have them for lunch, dinner and dessert!

parrish smith | lincoln, nebraska

3/4	cup water
3/4	cup milk
2	eggs
2	tablespoons butter, melted
1/2	teaspoon vanilla extract
1	cup all-purpose flour
1	tablespoon sugar
1/2	teaspoon salt

BANANA FILLING:

3	tablespoons butter
3	tablespoons brown sugar
3	medium, firm bananas, cut into 1/4-inch slices

SOUR CREAM FILLING:

1	cup (8 ounces) sour cream
2	tablespoons confectioners' sugar
1/2	cup slivered almonds, toasted

Additional confectioners' sugar and toasted almonds

In a small bowl, combine the water, milk, eggs, butter and vanilla. Combine the flour, sugar and salt; add to milk mixture and mix well. Cover and refrigerate for 1 hour.

Heat a lightly greased 8-in. nonstick skillet; pour 3 tablespoons batter into the center of skillet. Lift and tilt pan to evenly coat bottom.

Cook for 1-2 minutes until top appears dry; turn and cook 15-20 seconds longer. Remove to a wire rack. Repeat with remaining batter. When cool, stack crepes with waxed paper or paper towels in between.

For banana filling, in a small skillet, heat butter and brown sugar over medium heat until sugar is dissolved. Add bananas; toss to coat. Remove from the heat; keep warm.

For sour cream filling, in a small bowl, combine sour cream and confectioners' sugar. Spread over each crepe. Spoon banana filling over sour cream filling; sprinkle with almonds. Roll up crepes; sprinkle with additional confectioners' sugar and toasted almonds.

Breakfast TIP

To toast slivered almonds, heat a dry skillet until hot. Pour the almonds in and spread out in a single layer. Stir frequently and cook for 3-5 minutes.

PUFF PANCAKE WITH BLUEBERRY SAUCE

YIELD: 4 SERVINGS

I collect cookbooks and discovered this recipe while I was in Texas on vacation. The light and puffy pancake really does melt in your mouth! It's a definite crowd-pleaser that's as impressive served at dessert as it is at breakfast. My guests always agree!

barbara mohr | millington, michigan

2	tablespoons butter
2	eggs
1/2	cup milk
1/2	cup all-purpose flour
2	tablespoons sugar
1/8	teaspoon ground cinnamon

BLUEBERRY SAUCE:

1/4	cup packed brown sugar
1	tablespoon cornstarch
1/4	cup orange juice
1	cup fresh *or* frozen blueberries
1/4	teaspoon vanilla extract

Place butter in a 9-in. pie plate; place in a 425° oven for 4-5 minutes or until melted. Meanwhile, in a small bowl, whisk eggs and milk. In another small bowl, combine the flour, sugar and cinnamon; whisk in egg mixture until smooth. Pour into prepared pie plate. Bake for 18-22 minutes or until sides are crisp and golden brown.

Meanwhile, in a small saucepan, combine brown sugar and cornstarch. Gradually whisk in orange juice until smooth. Stir in blueberries. Bring to a boil over medium heat, stirring constantly. Cook and stir 1-2 minutes longer or until thickened. Remove from the heat; stir in vanilla. Serve the blueberry sauce with pancake.

PUFF PANCAKE WITH BLUEBERRY SAUCE

HAM 'N' CHEESE CREPES
YIELD: 4 FILLED CREPES PLUS 4 UNFILLED CREPES

These thin pancakes are easy to freeze and thaw. For two people, just cook up a batch, enjoy just enough for two and freeze the rest to savor for breakfast, dinner or another time.

marion lowery | medford, oregon

- 1/3   cup cold water
- 1/3   cup plus 2 to 3 tablespoons 2% milk, *divided*
- 1/2   cup all-purpose flour
- 1   egg
- 2   tablespoons butter, melted
- 1/8   teaspoon salt

ADDITIONAL INGREDIENTS (for 4 crepes):
- 1   tablespoon Dijon mustard
- 4   thin slices deli ham
- 1/2   cup shredded cheddar cheese

In a blender, combine the water, 1/3 cup milk, flour, egg, butter and salt; cover and process until smooth. Refrigerate batter for at least 30 minutes; stir. Add the remaining milk if the batter is too thick.

Heat a lightly greased 8-in. skillet; add about 3 tablespoons batter. Lift and tilt pan to evenly coat bottom. Cook until top appears dry; turn and cook 15-20 seconds longer. Repeat with remaining batter, greasing skillet as needed. Stack four crepes with waxed paper in between; cover and freeze for up to 3 months.

Spread mustard over remaining crepes; top each with ham and cheese. Roll up tightly. Place in an 8-in. square baking dish coated with cooking spray. Bake, uncovered, at 375° for 10-14 minutes or until heated through.

To use frozen crepes: Thaw in the refrigerator for about 2 hours. Fill and bake as directed.

HAM 'N' CHEESE CREPES

PUFFY OVEN PANCAKES

PUFFY OVEN PANCAKES
YIELD: 2 SERVINGS

Puffy and pretty, with a refreshing hint of lemon, this berry-topped pancake is a cherished favorite. What a melt-in-your-mouth morning wake-up or addition to a special brunch!

lillian julow | gainesville, florida

- 2   tablespoons butter, *divided*
- 2   eggs
- 1/2   cup 2% milk
- 1   teaspoon grated lemon peel
- 1/2   teaspoon vanilla extract
- 1/2   cup all-purpose flour
- 1/4   cup fresh blueberries
- 1/4   cup fresh raspberries
- 1/4   cup sliced fresh strawberries
- 1   teaspoon confectioners' sugar

Divide butter between two 2-cup round baking dishes. Place on a baking sheet. Heat in a 400° oven until butter is melted.

In a small bowl, whisk the eggs, milk, lemon peel and vanilla. Whisk in flour until blended. Pour over butter. Bake, uncovered, for 14-16 minutes or until golden brown and puffy.

Gently combine the berries. Spoon onto pancakes; sprinkle with confectioners' sugar. Serve immediately.

SWEET CORN BLINTZES
YIELD: 4 SERVINGS

I often make a double batch of these blintzes to take to work. I always come home with an empty platter!

paula marchesi | lenhartsville, pennsylvania

- 1/2   cup fat-free half-and-half
- 1   cup frozen corn, thawed
- 1/2   cup all-purpose flour
- 2   eggs

2 tablespoons butter, melted
1/2 teaspoon salt
1/4 teaspoon pepper
1-1/2 cups (12 ounces) 2% cottage cheese, drained
1/4 cup sugar
Confectioners' sugar, optional

Place the half-and-half and corn in a blender; cover and process until smooth. Add the flour, eggs, butter, salt and pepper; cover and process until blended. Cover batter and refrigerate for 1 hour.

Heat an 8-in. nonstick skillet coated with cooking spray; pour about 3 tablespoons batter into the center of skillet. Lift and tilt pan to evenly coat bottom. Cook until top appears dry; turn and cook 15-20 seconds longer. Remove to a wire rack. Repeat with remaining batter, using additional cooking spray as needed. When cool, stack crepes with waxed paper or paper towels in between.

In a small bowl, combine the cottage cheese and sugar. Spoon 2 tablespoonfuls down the center of each crepe; roll up. Place in a 13-in. x 9-in. baking dish. Bake, uncovered, at 350° for 8-10 minutes or until heated through. Sprinkle with confectioners' sugar if desired.

SWEET CORN BLINTZES

HEARTY HOTCAKES
YIELD: 16 HOTCAKES

I blend buttermilk with cornmeal and two kinds of flour for these filling pancakes that are sure to wake up your guests' taste buds. Oats give these golden hotcakes a unique crunch.

nancy horsburgh | everett, ontario

1 cup all-purpose flour
1/2 cup whole wheat flour
1/2 cup cornmeal
1/2 cup quick-cooking oats
2 tablespoons sugar
1/2 teaspoon baking powder
1/2 teaspoon baking soda
1/2 teaspoon salt
1 egg

2-1/2 cups buttermilk
3 tablespoons butter, melted
Maple syrup *or* topping of your choice

In a large bowl, combine the dry ingredients. In a small bowl, beat egg, buttermilk and butter; stir into dry ingredients just until moistened.

Pour batter by 1/4 cupfuls onto a lightly greased hot griddle; turn when bubbles form on top. Cook until second side is golden brown. Serve with syrup or topping of your choice.

GERMAN PANCAKE
YIELD: 8 SERVINGS (ABOUT 2 CUPS SYRUP)

Piping hot and puffy from the oven, this golden pancake made a pretty presentation for a skier's theme breakfast I hosted. Served with my homemade buttermilk syrup, it's an eye-opening treat. That easy syrup tastes great on waffles and French toast, too.

renae moncur | burley, idaho

6 eggs
1 cup milk
1 cup all-purpose flour
1/2 teaspoon salt
2 tablespoons butter, melted
BUTTERMILK SYRUP:
1-1/2 cups sugar
3/4 cup buttermilk
1/2 cup butter
2 tablespoons corn syrup
1 teaspoon baking soda
2 teaspoons vanilla extract
Confectioners' sugar

In a blender, combine the eggs, milk, flour and salt; cover and process until smooth.

Pour the butter into an ungreased 13-in. x 9-in. baking dish; add the batter. Bake, uncovered, at 400° for 20 minutes.

Meanwhile, for syrup, in a small saucepan, combine the first five syrup ingredients; bring to a boil. Boil for 7 minutes. Remove from the heat; stir in vanilla. Dust pancake with confectioners' sugar; serve immediately with the syrup.

Breakfast TIP

Here's a unique way to prepare pancakes for a crowd. My daughter-in-law pours the batter onto a cookie sheet and bakes it at 400° for about 20 minutes. She then cuts the giant pancake into squares. You could also use large circle cookie cutters.

—Ruth G., Menominee, Michigan

WAFFLES & FRENCH TOAST

MAKE MORNINGS
SPECIAL WITH THIS
SCRUMPTIOUS
ASSORTMENT OF
FRENCH TOAST
AND WAFFLE
FAVORITES.

APRICOT-COCONUT
FRENCH TOAST
PAGE 49

For homemade freezer waffles, bake and cool on a wire rack. Then freeze waffles in a single layer on a baking sheet. When frozen, store in heavy-duty freezer bags.

For French toast that's ready on the fly, prepare as directed. Then once cool, wrap the slices in serving-size portions and freeze. When ready to use, pop the waffles or French toast into the toaster or toaster oven to defrost and reheat.

WAFFLES WITH PEACH-BERRY COMPOTE

This recipe was created one summer Sunday morning when I was looking for a more healthful alternative to butter and maple syrup to top my waffles. I was amazed at the results!

brandi waters | fayetteville, arkansas

WAFFLES WITH PEACH-BERRY COMPOTE
YIELD: 12 WAFFLES (1-1/2 CUPS COMPOTE)

1 cup chopped peeled fresh peaches *or* frozen unsweetened sliced peaches, thawed and chopped
1/2 cup orange juice
2 tablespoons brown sugar
1/4 teaspoon ground cinnamon
1 cup fresh *or* frozen blueberries
1/2 cup sliced fresh *or* frozen strawberries

BATTER:
1-1/4 cups all-purpose flour
1/2 cup whole wheat flour
2 tablespoons flaxseed
1 teaspoon baking powder
1 teaspoon baking soda
1/2 teaspoon ground cinnamon
1 cup buttermilk
3/4 cup orange juice
1 tablespoon canola oil
1 teaspoon vanilla extract

In a small saucepan, combine the peaches, orange juice, brown sugar and cinnamon; bring to a boil over medium heat. Add berries; cook and stir for 8-10 minutes or until thickened.

For batter, in a large bowl, combine the flours, flaxseed, baking powder, baking soda and cinnamon. Combine the buttermilk, orange juice, oil and vanilla; stir into dry ingredients just until moistened.

Bake in a preheated waffle iron according to manufacturer's directions until golden brown. Serve with compote.

BLUEBERRY FRENCH TOAST

BLUEBERRY FRENCH TOAST
YIELD: 6 SERVINGS

1/2	cup sugar
2-1/2	teaspoons cornstarch
1	teaspoon ground cinnamon
1/4	teaspoon ground allspice
3/4	cup water
4	cups fresh *or* frozen blueberries
1	cup egg substitute
1	cup fat-free milk
1	teaspoon vanilla extract
1/2	teaspoon salt
12	slices French bread (1 inch thick)

In a large bowl, combine the sugar, cornstarch, cinnamon and allspice; stir in water until smooth. Add blueberries; mix well. Transfer to a 13-in. x 9-in. baking dish coated with cooking spray.

In a large bowl, beat the egg substitute, milk, vanilla and salt. Dip each slice of bread into egg mixture; arrange slices over berries. Bake at 400° for 20-25 minutes or until toast is golden brown and blueberries are bubbly.

The original recipe for this French toast called for heavy cream and whole eggs, but I decided to try my hand at lightening it up and still keeping the delicious taste. This was a success!

nancy argo | uniontown, ohio

STRAWBERRY-TOPPED WAFFLES
YIELD: 6-8 WAFFLES

2	pints fresh strawberries
5	tablespoons sugar, *divided*
2	cups all-purpose flour
2	teaspoons baking powder
1/2	teaspoon baking soda
1/2	teaspoon salt
2	eggs
2	cups (16 ounces) sour cream
1	cup milk
3	tablespoons canola oil

Whipped topping *or* vanilla ice cream
Additional strawberries, optional

Place the strawberries and 3 tablespoons of sugar in a food processor or blender. Cover and process until coarsely chopped; set aside.

In a large bowl, combine the flour, baking powder, baking soda, salt and remaining sugar. In another bowl, combine the eggs, sour cream, milk and oil; stir into dry ingredients just until combined.

Preheat waffle iron. Fill and bake according to manufacturer's directions. Serve waffles with strawberry topping, whipped topping and additional strawberries if desired.

STRAWBERRY-TOPPED WAFFLES

Topped with a sweet strawberry sauce, these tender from-scratch waffles will make the first meal of the day something truly special.

sue mackey | galesburg, illinois

CHEDDAR FRENCH TOAST WITH DRIED FRUIT SYRUP
YIELD: 6 SERVINGS

My family loves this warm French toast on cold mornings in the North Carolina mountains where we vacation each year. Feel free to experiment with different dried fruits in the syrup.

jackie lintz | cocoa beach, florida

1-1/2	cups maple syrup
1	package (8 ounces) dried fruit, diced
1/4	cup chopped walnuts
12	slices Italian *or* French bread (cut diagonally 1 inch thick)
1-1/3	cups shredded sharp cheddar cheese
4	eggs
2	cups milk
1/4	teaspoon salt

In a large bowl, combine the syrup, dried fruit and walnuts; cover and let stand overnight.

Cut a slit in the crust of each slice of bread to form a pocket. Stuff each pocket with 2 tablespoons cheese. In a large bowl, whisk the eggs, milk and salt; soak bread for 2 minutes per side. Cook on a greased hot griddle until golden brown on both sides. Serve with dried fruit syrup.

CHEDDAR FRENCH TOAST WITH DRIED FRUIT SYRUP

CHERRY-GRANOLA FRENCH TOAST STICKS

CHERRY-GRANOLA FRENCH TOAST STICKS
YIELD: 4 SERVINGS

The warm aroma of cinnamon and brown sugar helps wake my family. These convenient French toast sticks topped with granola, banana and whipped cream carry them through busy mornings.

terri mckitrick | delafield, wisconsin

1/4	cup heavy whipping cream
3	tablespoons brown sugar
2	tablespoons butter
1	tablespoon dried cherries
1/4	teaspoon ground cinnamon
1/4	teaspoon vanilla extract
1	package (12.7 ounces) frozen French toast sticks
1	medium banana, sliced
1/4	cup granola without raisins

In a small saucepan, combine the cream, brown sugar, butter, cherries and cinnamon. Bring to a boil over medium heat, stirring constantly. Cook and stir for 2 minutes. Remove from the heat; stir in vanilla.

Prepare French toast sticks according to package directions. Serve with banana, granola and syrup.

EDITOR'S NOTE: This recipe was tested with Eggo French Toaster Sticks.

HAWAIIAN WAFFLES
YIELD: 16 (4-INCH) WAFFLES

I created this dish to recapture the tropical tastes we enjoyed while visiting Hawaii. Featuring the flavors of pineapple, coconut and macadamia nuts, it's a wonderful morning starter.

darlene brenden | salem, oregon

1	can (20 ounces) crushed pineapple, undrained
1/2	cup sugar
1/2	cup flaked coconut
1/2	cup light corn syrup
1/4	cup pineapple juice

WAFFLES:

2	cups all-purpose flour
4	teaspoons baking powder
1	tablespoon sugar
1/2	teaspoon salt
2	eggs, *separated*
1	cup milk
1/4	cup butter, melted
1	can (8 ounces) crushed pineapple, well drained
1/4	cup flaked coconut
1/4	cup chopped macadamia nuts

Additional chopped macadamia nuts, toasted, optional

In a large saucepan, combine the first five ingredients. Bring to a boil. Reduce heat. Simmer, uncovered, for 12-15 minutes or until sauce begins to thicken; set aside.

For waffles, in a large bowl, combine the flour, baking powder, sugar and salt. Combine egg yolks, milk and butter; stir into dry ingredients just until combined. Stir in pineapple, coconut and nuts. Beat egg whites until stiff peaks form; fold into batter (batter will be thick).

Preheat waffle iron. Fill and bake according to manufacturer's directions. Serve with pineapple sauce and additional nuts if desired.

HAWAIIAN WAFFLES

FRENCH TOAST SUPREME

FRENCH TOAST SUPREME
YIELD: 4-6 SERVINGS

As teachers, my husband and I rarely have time for breakfast during the week. So we look forward to relaxing breakfasts with our daughters on weekends. The cinnamon bread used in this deliciously different recipe is a nice variation.

janis hoople | stanton, michigan

3	eggs
1/4	cup milk
1	tablespoon sugar
1	teaspoon vanilla extract
1	carton (4 ounces) whipped cream cheese
12	slices cinnamon bread

Kiwifruit and starfruit, optional

In a bowl, beat eggs, milk, sugar and vanilla. Spread 1 tablespoon cream cheese on six slices bread; top with remaining slices to make six sandwiches.

Dip sandwiches in egg mixture. Fry on a lightly greased skillet until golden brown on both sides. Garnish with kiwi and starfruit if desired.

EGGNOG FRENCH TOAST
YIELD: 8-10 SERVINGS

This recipe is one of my family's favorites not only at Christmas but any time of the year. We especially like to prepare it when we go camping. It gives the day a healthy beginning.

robert northrup | las cruces, new mexico

8	eggs
2	cups eggnog
1/4	cup sugar
1/2	teaspoon vanilla *or* rum extract
20	to 26 slices English muffin bread

Confectioners' sugar, optional

Maple syrup

In a bowl, beat eggs, eggnog, sugar and extract; soak bread for 2 minutes per side. Cook on a greased hot griddle until golden brown on both sides and cooked through. Dust with confectioners' sugar if desired. Serve with syrup.

LIGHT 'N' CRISPY WAFFLES
YIELD: 12 WAFFLES

Our home economists added club soda to give these waffles a fluffy texture. With only four ingredients, making homemade waffles don't get any easier!

taste of home test kitchen

2 cups biscuit/baking mix
2 eggs, lightly beaten
1/2 cup canola oil
1 cup club soda

In a large bowl, combine the biscuit mix, eggs and oil. Add club soda and stir until smooth.

Bake in a preheated waffle iron according to manufacturer's directions until golden brown.

LIGHT 'N' CRISPY WAFFLES

OATMEAL WAFFLES
YIELD: 12 WAFFLES (4-INCHES SQUARE EACH), ABOUT 6 SERVINGS

These healthful, good-tasting waffles are a tried-and-true family favorite—even with our two children. While they taste wonderful drizzled with maple syrup, we prefer them topped with fresh fruit or berries and yogurt.

marna heitz | farley, iowa

1-1/2 cups all-purpose flour
1 cup quick-cooking oats
3 teaspoons baking powder
1/2 teaspoon ground cinnamon
1/4 teaspoon salt, optional
2 eggs, lightly beaten
1-1/2 cups milk

6 tablespoons butter, melted
2 tablespoons brown sugar
Fresh fruit and yogurt, optional

In large bowl, combine the flour, oats, baking powder, cinnamon and salt; set aside. In small bowl, whisk the eggs, milk, butter and brown sugar. Add to flour mixture; stir until blended.

Pour batter into a lightly greased waffle iron (amount will vary with size of waffle iron). Close lid quickly; do not open during baking. Use fork to remove baked waffle. Top with fresh fruit and yogurt if desired.

FRENCH TOAST SANDWICHES
YIELD: 6 SERVINGS

I dip these yummy breakfast sandwiches into eggnog to give them a distinctive flavor that's perfect for the holidays. They have become a tasty holiday tradition for our family.

deborah fagan | lancaster, pennsylvania

12 slices Canadian bacon
6 slices Monterey Jack cheese
12 slices French bread (1/2 inch thick)
3/4 cup eggnog
3 tablespoons butter
6 tablespoons strawberry preserves

Place two slices of Canadian bacon and one slice of cheese on each of six slices of bread. Top with remaining bread. Place eggnog in a shallow dish. Dip sandwiches in eggnog.

In a large skillet or griddle, melt 2-3 tablespoons butter. Toast sandwiches until bread is lightly browned on both sides, adding butter if necessary. Serve with strawberry preserves.

EDITOR'S NOTE: This recipe was tested with

FRENCH TOAST SANDWICHES

VERY VANILLA FRENCH TOAST

VERY VANILLA FRENCH TOAST
YIELD: 4 SERVINGS

The decadent toast slices boast a creamy vanilla flavor from convenient pudding mix, plus a hint of cinnamon. We like to top this with syrup or powdered sugar and fresh berries. As a change of pace, try butterscotch pudding instead.

linda bernhagen | plainfield, illinois

1	cup milk
1	package (3 ounces) cook-and-serve vanilla pudding mix
1	egg
1/2	teaspoon ground cinnamon
8	slices Texas toast
2	teaspoons butter

In a large bowl, whisk the milk, vanilla pudding mix, egg and cinnamon for 2 minutes or until well blended. Dip toast in pudding mixture, coating both sides.

In a large skillet, melt butter over medium heat. Cook bread on both sides until golden brown.

TRUE BELGIAN WAFFLES
YIELD: 10 WAFFLES (ABOUT 4-1/2 INCHES)

It was on a visit to my husband's relatives in Belgium that I was given this recipe. Back in the U.S., I served the waffles to his Belgian-born grandmother. She said they tasted just like home. The grandkids love these waffles with just about any kind of topping, such as blueberries, strawberries, raspberries, cinnamon, fried apples, powdered sugar or whipped topping.

rose delemeester | st. charles, michigan

2	cups all-purpose flour
3/4	cup sugar
3-1/2	teaspoons baking powder
2	eggs, *separated*

1-1/2	cups milk
1	cup butter, melted
1	teaspoon vanilla extract

Sliced fresh strawberries *or* syrup

In a bowl, combine flour, sugar and baking powder. In another bowl, lightly beat egg yolks. Add milk, butter and vanilla; mix well. Stir into dry ingredients just until combined. Beat egg whites until stiff peaks form; fold into batter.

Bake in a preheated waffle iron according to manufacturer's directions until golden brown. Serve with strawberries or syrup.

COTTAGE CHEESE WAFFLES
YIELD: 4 WAFFLES (6-1/2 INCHES)

Cottage cheese and extra eggs make these waffles soft and moist, with a different texture than other versions. Topped with real maple syrup, this is my family's favorite Sunday breakfast.

lisabeth hess | chambersburg, pennsylvania

1	cup (8 ounces) cream-style cottage cheese, undrained
6	eggs
1/4	cup canola oil
1/2	teaspoon vanilla extract
1/2	cup all-purpose flour
1/4	teaspoon salt

Maple syrup

In a blender, combine the cottage cheese, eggs, oil and vanilla. Cover and process until well combined. Add flour and salt; process until smooth.

Bake in a preheated waffle iron according to manufacturer's directions until golden brown. Serve with syrup.

COTTAGE CHEESE WAFFLES

APRICOT-COCONUT FRENCH TOAST
YIELD: 8 SERVINGS

As a busy activity director in RV parks, I was always looking for easy food to prepare for various functions. This breakfast dish always brought raves. Leftovers, if there are any, are wonderful. Just pop slices in the microwave for 15 seconds each.

jean groen | *apache junction, arizona*

1/2	cup chopped dried apricots
1/2	cup water
1/4	cup butter, melted
2/3	cup flaked coconut, toasted
1/4	cup sugar
1-1/4	teaspoons ground cinnamon
7	eggs
1-3/4	cups milk
1	teaspoon vanilla extract

Pinch salt

16	slices French bread (1 inch thick)

Maple syrup

In a small microwave-safe bowl, heat apricots and water on high for 2 minutes or until mixture comes to a boil. Let stand for 5 minutes; drain.

Pour butter into a 15-in. x 10-in. baking pan and tilt to coat bottom. Sprinkle with coconut and apricots. Combine sugar and cinnamon; sprinkle over fruit.

In a large shallow bowl, whisk the eggs, milk, vanilla extract and salt. Dip bread into egg mixture; soak for 1 minute. Place the slices close together over the coconut mixture. Cover and refrigerate overnight.

Remove from the refrigerator 30 minutes before baking. Bake, uncovered, at 375° for 20-25 minutes or until golden brown. Serve with syrup.

EDITOR'S NOTE: A dark baking pan is not recommended for this recipe.

COCONUT FRENCH TOAST
YIELD: 7 SERVINGS

The scrumptious fare is made deliciously unique by first soaking the bread in a simple egg mixture, rolling in sweet coconut, then baking.

charlotte baillargeon | *hinsdale, massachusetts*

12	eggs
1-1/4	cups milk
2	teaspoons sugar
1	teaspoon ground cinnamon
14	slices day-old bread
1	package (7 ounces) flaked coconut

Maple syrup

In a large bowl, beat eggs; add milk, sugar and cinnamon. Add bread, a few slices at a time; let soak for 1 minute on each side. Coat both sides with coconut. Place on greased baking sheets.

Bake at 475° for 5 minutes on each side or until golden brown and cooked through. Serve with syrup.

WILD RICE PECAN WAFFLES
YIELD: 5-6 WAFFLES (ABOUT 6-1/2 INCHES)

My mother found this recipe and shared it with me. It has become a family treasure, especially when the hearty, nutty waffles are served with my dad's homemade maple syrup.

kris sackett | *eau claire, wisconsin*

1	cup all-purpose flour
1	teaspoon baking powder
1/2	teaspoon salt
2	eggs, *separated*
2/3	cup milk
1/4	cup canola oil
1-1/2	cups cooked wild rice
1/2	cup chopped pecans

In a large bowl, combine the flour, baking powder and salt. In a small bowl, whisk the egg yolks, milk and oil. Stir into dry ingredients just until moistened. In another bowl, beat egg whites until stiff peaks form; fold into batter. Fold in the wild rice and pecans.

Bake in a preheated greased waffle iron according to manufacturer's directions until golden brown.

Breakfast TIP

I've found a tasty replacement for the syrup and butter that I used to put on top of my waffles. I now mix equal parts of fat-free fruit-flavored yogurt with fat-free whipped topping. This also makes a refreshing fruit dip.

—Elaine C., Afton, Wyoming

PEACH-STUFFED FRENCH TOAST
YIELD: 10 SERVINGS

With its make-ahead convenience and scrumptious flavor, this recipe is ideal for holiday brunches or for busy hostesses with a hungry crowd to feed! This is truly a standout dish.

julie robinson | little chute, wisconsin

    1   loaf (1 pound) French bread, cut into 20 slices
    1   can (15 ounces) sliced peaches in extra-light
        syrup, drained and chopped
  1/4   cup chopped pecans
    4   eggs
    4   egg whites
1-1/2   cups milk
    3   tablespoons sugar
1-1/4   teaspoons ground cinnamon, *divided*
    1   teaspoon vanilla extract
  1/4   cup all-purpose flour
    2   tablespoons brown sugar
    2   tablespoons cold butter
Maple syrup, optional

Arrange half of the bread in a 13-in. x 9-in. baking dish coated with cooking spray. Top with the chopped peaches, pecans and the remaining bread.

In a small bowl, whisk the eggs, egg whites, milk, sugar, 1 teaspoon cinnamon and vanilla; pour over bread. Cover and refrigerate for 8 hours or overnight.

Remove from the refrigerator 30 minutes before baking. Bake, uncovered, at 400° for 20 minutes.

In a small bowl, combine the flour, brown sugar and remaining cinnamon; cut in butter until crumbly. Sprinkle crumb mixture over French toast. Bake 5-10 minutes longer or until a knife inserted near the center comes out clean. Serve French toast with syrup if desired.

PEACH-STUFFED FRENCH TOAST

WAFFLES WITH VANILLA SAUCE

WAFFLES WITH VANILLA SAUCE
YIELD: 6-8 WAFFLES (6-1/2 INCHES)

I like to serve these flavorful waffles when we have company because they add nice color to the table and look so elegant, yet they're so easy to prepare. Everyone raves about the rich, creamy vanilla sauce served over the warm waffles.

sandra falk | steinbach, michigan

1-2/3   cups all-purpose flour
    4   teaspoons baking powder
  1/2   teaspoon salt
    2   eggs, *separated*
3-2/3   cups milk, *divided*
    6   tablespoons canola oil
  1/2   cup sugar
    1   teaspoon vanilla extract
Fresh strawberries

In a bowl, combine flour, baking powder and salt. In another bowl, beat egg yolks lightly. Add 1-2/3 cups milk and oil; stir into dry ingredients just until moistened. Set aside 1/4 cup batter in a small bowl. Beat egg whites until stiff peaks form; fold into remaining batter.

Bake in a preheated waffle iron according to manufacturer's directions until golden brown.

In a saucepan, heat sugar and remaining milk until scalded. Stir a small amount into reserved batter; return all to pan. Bring to a boil; boil for 5-7 minutes or until thickened. Remove from the heat; add vanilla and mix well (sauce will thicken upon standing). Serve over waffles. Top with berries.

OAT WAFFLES
YIELD: 8 WAFFLES (ABOUT 6-1/2 INCHES)

These golden delights have more fiber and less fat than standard waffles. My daughter loves them with fresh berries.

karen hayes | danville, virginia

1   cup all-purpose flour
1   cup oat flour
4   teaspoons baking powder
1   tablespoon sugar
1/2 teaspoon salt
2   eggs
1-3/4 cups milk
2   tablespoons canola oil
1   teaspoon vanilla extract

In a large bowl, combine the first five ingredients. Combine the eggs, milk, oil and vanilla; stir into dry ingredients just until combined.

Pour batter by 1/2 cupfuls into a preheated waffle iron; bake according to manufacturer's directions until golden brown.

EDITOR'S NOTE: As a substitute for the oat flour, process 1-1/4 cups quick-cooking oats until finely ground.

FRUITY FRENCH TOAST
YIELD: 2 SERVINGS

My son begged me to try making the stuffed French toast we enjoyed when our family visited Walt Disney World. His encouragement resulted in this easy delicious breakfast that's a favorite on Saturday morning.

nancy hawthorne | gettysburg, pennsylvania

1   medium firm banana, sliced
4   slices Texas toast
2   teaspoons confectioners' sugar, *divided*
2   large strawberries, sliced
1   egg
1/2 cup milk
1/2 teaspoon vanilla extract
1/4 teaspoon ground cinnamon
2   teaspoons butter
Maple syrup

FRUITY FRENCH TOAST

Place banana slices on two slices of toast. Sprinkle each with 1/2 teaspoon confectioners' sugar. Top with strawberries and remaining toast. In a shallow bowl, whisk the egg, milk, vanilla and cinnamon. Dip toast in egg mixture, coating both sides.

In a large skillet, melt butter over medium heat; cook toast for 2-4 minutes on each side or until golden brown. Sprinkle with remaining confectioners' sugar. Serve with maple syrup.

PECAN CHOCOLATE WAFFLES

PECAN CHOCOLATE WAFFLES
YIELD: 8 WAFFLES

If you like waffles and chocolate, this recipe is for you. These tender but crunchy waffles are great for breakfast, brunch or an after-dinner dessert. If you like, instead of chocolate topping, top with berries and whipped cream or simply sprinkle with powdered sugar.

agnes golian | garfield heights, ohio

1   cup pancake mix
1   egg
3/4 cup 2% milk
1/4 cup chocolate syrup
2   tablespoons canola oil
1/3 cup chopped pecans
CHOCOLATE BUTTER:
1/4 cup butter, softened
1/4 cup confectioners' sugar
1   tablespoon baking cocoa

Place pancake mix in a bowl. In another bowl, whisk the egg, milk, chocolate syrup and oil. Stir into pancake mix just until combined. Stir in pecans.

Bake in a preheated waffle iron according to manufacturer's directions until golden brown. Meanwhile, in a small bowl, beat chocolate butter ingredients until smooth. Serve with waffles.

CROISSANT FRENCH TOAST
YIELD: 4 SERVINGS

More like a scrumptious dessert than a main dish, this rich version of French toast is topped with tangy raspberry and smooth vanilla sauces that use ice cream. I cut the croissants into shapes with a cookie cutter for my grandson. He even asks for the "ice cream sauce" on his pancakes.

june dickerson | *philippi, west virginia*

- 1/2 cup sugar
- 1 tablespoon all-purpose flour
- 2 cups heavy whipping cream
- 4 egg yolks
- 1 tablespoon vanilla extract
- 2 scoops vanilla ice cream

BERRY SAUCE:
- 2 cups fresh raspberries *or* frozen unsweetened raspberries
- 2 tablespoons sugar

FRENCH TOAST:
- 3 eggs
- 4 croissants, split
- 2 tablespoons butter

In a large saucepan, combine the sugar and flour. Stir in cream until smooth. Cook and stir over medium-high heat until thickened and bubbly. Reduce heat; cook and stir 2 minutes longer. Remove from the heat. Stir a small amount of hot filling into egg yolks; return all to the pan, stirring constantly. Cook and stir until mixture reaches 160°.

Remove from the heat. Gently stir in vanilla and ice cream until the ice cream is melted. Place plastic wrap over the surface of the sauce; cool.

For berry sauce, combine the raspberries and sugar in a saucepan. Simmer, uncovered, for 2-3 minutes. Remove from the heat; set aside.

For French toast, in a shallow bowl, beat eggs. Dip both sides of croissants in egg mixture. On a griddle, brown croissants on both sides in butter. Serve with vanilla and berry sauces.

CROISSANT FRENCH TOAST

BUTTERMILK WAFFLES

BUTTERMILK WAFFLES
YIELD: 16 WAFFLES (4 INCHES)

You won't get any complaints from family or friends when you stack up these golden waffles on a platter. This is a popular morning mainstay that my gang requests regularly.

kim branges | *grand canyon, arizona*

- 1-3/4 cups all-purpose flour
- 1 teaspoon baking powder
- 1 teaspoon baking soda
- 1/2 teaspoon salt
- 2 eggs
- 2 cups buttermilk
- 1/3 cup canola oil

Strawberry pancake syrup and whipped cream, optional

In a large bowl, combine the flour, baking powder, baking soda and salt. In another bowl, beat the eggs; add buttermilk and oil. Stir into dry ingredients just until combined.

Bake in a preheated waffle iron according to manufacturer's directions until golden brown. Serve waffles with syrup and whipped cream if desired.

CANADIAN BACON WAFFLES
YIELD: 12 WAFFLES

Our home economists cut prep time for this recipe by relying on a biscuit/baking mix. Mixing Canadian bacon into the batter makes these waffles a satisfying meal-in-one.

taste of home test kitchen

- 2 cups biscuit/baking mix
- 2 eggs, lightly beaten
- 1/2 cup canola oil
- 1 cup club soda
- 1/2 cup chopped Canadian bacon
- 1/2 cup shredded cheddar cheese
- 1 teaspoon minced chives

In a small bowl, combine the biscuit mix, eggs and oil. Add club soda and stir until smooth. Gently fold in the Canadian bacon, cheese and chives.

Bake in a preheated waffle iron according to manufacturer's directions until golden brown.

CRISPY FRENCH TOAST

CRISPY FRENCH TOAST
YIELD: 12 SLICES

I lightened up this golden French toast with egg substitute and skim milk, then flavored it with orange juice, vanilla and a dash of nutmeg. The cornflake coating adds a fun crunch.

flo burtnett | gage, oklahoma

1/2   cup egg substitute
1/2   cup fat-free milk
1/4   cup orange juice
1   teaspoon vanilla extract
Dash ground nutmeg
12   slices day-old French bread (3/4 inch thick)
1-1/2 cups crushed cornflakes

In a shallow dish, combine the egg substitute, milk, orange juice, vanilla and nutmeg. Add bread; soak for 5 minutes, turning once. Coat both sides of each slice with cornflake crumbs.

Place in a 15-in. x 10-in. baking pan coated with cooking spray. Bake at 425° for 10 minutes; turn. Bake 5-8 minutes longer or until golden brown.

Breakfast TIP

After pouring the batter into the waffle iron, I like to sprinkle on crushed potato chips for extra crunch.

—Mrs. Elwin E., Salem, Oregon

SWEET CHERRY FRENCH TOAST
YIELD: 4 SERVINGS

You'll be proud to serve this tasty brunch bake. The sweet cherry topping and dollop of yogurt make each bite a special treat.

elisa lochridge | tigard, oregon

8   slices French bread (1 inch thick)
6   eggs
1-1/2 cups milk
1/3   cup maple syrup
3   tablespoons sugar, *divided*
1   tablespoon grated orange peel
1/8   teaspoon salt
4   cups fresh *or* frozen pitted sweet cherries
1/2   cup orange juice
4   teaspoons cornstarch
4   teaspoons cold water
Vanilla yogurt

Place the bread in a greased 15-in. x 10-in. baking pan. In a large bowl, whisk the eggs, milk, syrup, 2 tablespoons sugar, orange peel and salt. Pour over bread; turn to coat. Cover and refrigerate overnight. In another large bowl, combine the cherries, orange juice and remaining sugar. Cover and refrigerate overnight.

Transfer bread slices to another greased 15-in. x 10-in. baking pan. Discard any remaining egg mixture. Bake at 400° for 7-9 minutes or until golden brown.

Meanwhile, in a small saucepan, combine cornstarch and water until smooth. Stir in the reserved cherry mixture. Bring to a boil; cook and stir for 2 minutes or until thickened. Serve over French toast; drizzle with yogurt.

SWEET CHERRY FRENCH TOAST

BREAKFAST TO GO

THERE'S ALWAYS TIME FOR A HEARTY BREAKFAST THANKS TO THE HANDHELD MORNING FARE SHOWCASED HERE.

ORANGE PEACH SMOOTHIES
PAGE 63

Nothing beats egg, sausage and cheese on an English muffin. But since my husband and I both work, there isn't enough time to make these tasty breakfast sandwiches. Instead, I prepare a week's worth of the sandwiches on the weekend and store them individually in the freezer.

We simply put two sandwiches in the refrigerator the night before and pop them in the microwave the next morning.

—Terri V.,
St. Germain, Wisconsin

HAM 'N' EGG WRAPS

This is our favorite way to serve up eggs. Wrapped in a warm flour tortilla, eggs get extra-special treatment with the addition of ham, cheese and salsa.

marlene zimmerman | goshen, indiana

HAM 'N' EGG WRAPS
YIELD: 2 SERVINGS

4	eggs
1/2	teaspoon salt
1	tablespoon butter
1/2	cup chopped fully cooked ham
1/2	cup shredded cheddar cheese, *divided*
1/4	cup salsa
2	flour tortillas (10 inches), warmed

In a small bowl, whisk the eggs and salt. In a large skillet, heat butter until hot. Add egg mixture; cook and stir over medium heat until eggs are partially set. Add the ham, 1/4 cup shredded cheddar cheese and salsa; cook and stir until the eggs are completely set.

Spoon egg mixture off-center on each tortilla; sprinkle with remaining cheese. Fold sides and ends over filling and roll up.

GRANOLA BANANA STICKS

My daughter and I won an award at our local fair for these healthy morning snacks. I like to assemble the ingredients ahead for my kids to whip up when they get home from school. Sometimes we substitute rice cereal as a crunchy alternative to the crushed granola bars.

diane toomey | allentown, pennsylvania

GRANOLA BANANA STICKS
YIELD: 6 SERVINGS

1/4	cup peanut butter
2	tablespoons plus 1-1/2 teaspoons honey
4-1/2	teaspoons brown sugar
2	teaspoons milk
3	medium firm bananas
6	Popsicle sticks
2	crunchy oat and honey granola bars, crushed

In a small saucepan, combine the peanut butter, honey, brown sugar and milk; cook until heated through, stirring occasionally.

Peel bananas and cut in half widthwise; insert a Popsicle stick into one end of each banana half. Spoon peanut butter mixture over bananas to coat completely. Sprinkle with granola. Serve immediately or place on a waxed paper-lined baking sheet and freeze.

MINI SAUSAGE QUICHES
YIELD: 4 DOZEN

1/2	pound bulk hot Italian sausage
2	tablespoons dried minced onion
2	tablespoons minced chives
1	tube (8 ounces) refrigerated crescent rolls
4	eggs, lightly beaten
2	cups (8 ounces) shredded Swiss cheese
1	cup (8 ounces) 4% cottage cheese
1/3	cup grated Parmesan cheese

Paprika

In a large skillet, brown sausage and onion over medium heat for 4-5 minutes or until meat is no longer pink; drain. Stir in chives.

On a lightly floured surface, unroll crescent dough into one long rectangle; seal seams and perforations. Cut dough into 48 pieces. Press onto the bottom and up the sides of greased miniature muffin cups. Fill each with about 2 teaspoons of the sausage mixture. In a large bowl, combine the eggs and cheeses. Spoon 2 teaspoonfuls cheese mixture over sausage mixture. Sprinkle with paprika.

Bake at 375° for 20-25 minutes or until a knife inserted in the center comes out clean. Cool for 5 minutes before removing from pans to wire racks. Serve warm. Refrigerate leftovers.

MINI SAUSAGE QUICHES

These bite-size quiches are loaded with sausage and cheese, plus their crescent roll bases make preparation a snap. Serve these cute "muffinettes" at any brunch or potluck gathering.

jan mead | milford, connecticut

Fold points toward center and pinch edges to seal. Place on a lightly greased baking sheet. Bake at 375° for 11-13 minutes or until lightly browned.

BERRY BEST SMOOTHIES

BERRY BEST SMOOTHIES
YIELD: 3 SERVINGS

This fun recipe is a wonderful way to use up over-ripened bananas and to help my family get the required daily servings of fruit. It's so quick, easy and filling treat my kids absolutely love.

pamela klim | bettendorf, iowa

3	tablespoons orange juice concentrate
3	tablespoons fat-free half-and-half
12	ice cubes
1	cup fresh strawberries, hulled
1	medium ripe banana, cut into chunks
1/2	cup fresh *or* frozen blueberries
1/2	cup fresh *or* frozen raspberries

In a blender, combine all ingredients; cover and process for 30-45 seconds or until smooth. Pour into chilled glasses; serve immediately.

HAM 'N' SWISS ROLLS
YIELD: 4 SERVINGS (2 ROLLS EACH)

I depend on no-fuss recipes in planning breakfast for my husband and me. These portable, handheld rolls are perfect for families on the go and busy mornings.

marjorie carey | freeport, florida

1	tube (8 ounces) refrigerated crescent rolls
1	cup diced fully cooked ham
3/4	cup finely shredded Swiss cheese
1-1/2	teaspoons prepared mustard
1	teaspoon finely chopped onion

Separate crescent rolls into eight triangles. In a small bowl, combine the ham, cheese, mustard and onion; place 2 table-spoons mixture in the center of each triangle.

HEARTY BRUNCH POCKETS
YIELD: 6 SERVINGS

I made this recipe up when I was looking for a speedy and tasty meal for myself and my kids. These savory, handheld pockets filled with sausage, bacon, egg and cheese were an instant hit! I've learned they make a great meal any time of the day.

meredith beyl | stillwater, oklahoma

6	brown-and-serve sausage links, sliced
6	ready-to-serve fully cooked bacon strips, diced
6	eggs
2	tablespoons milk
1	teaspoon salt
1/4	teaspoon pepper
1	cup (4 ounces) shredded Colby-Monterey Jack cheese
3	pita breads (6 inches), halved

In a nonstick skillet, cook sausage for 2 minutes. Add bacon; cook 4 minutes longer or until sausage is heated through and bacon is crisp. Remove and keep warm.

In a small bowl, whisk the eggs, milk, salt and pepper. Pour into the skillet; cook and stir over medium heat until eggs are almost set. Add sausage mixture and cheese. Cook and stir for 2 minutes or until eggs are completely set and cheese is melted. Spoon into pita halves.

HEARTY BRUNCH POCKETS

BACON 'N' EGG BURRITOS
YIELD: 10 BURRITOS

To steer clear of hunger, I simply zap one of these frozen morning morsels in the microwave. The handheld breakfast starts my day right. This is my family's favorite combination, but you can replace the bacon with cooked breakfast sausage.

audra niederman | aberdeen, south dakota

    12   bacon strips, diced
    12   eggs, lightly beaten
Salt and pepper to taste
    10   flour tortillas (8 inches)
  1-1/2   cups (6 ounces) shredded cheddar cheese
   1/2   cup thinly sliced green onions

In a large skillet, cook bacon until crisp; remove to paper towels. Drain, reserving 1-2 tablespoons drippings. Add eggs, salt and pepper to drippings; cook and stir over medium heat until the eggs are completely set.

Spoon about 1/4 cup of egg mixture down the center of each tortilla; sprinkle with cheese, onions and reserved bacon. Fold bottom and sides of each tortilla over filling. Wrap each in waxed paper and aluminum foil. Freeze for up to 1 month.

To use frozen burritos: Remove foil. Place waxed paper-wrapped burritos on a microwave-safe plate. Microwave at 60% power for 1 to 1-1/2 minutes or until heated through. Let stand for 20 seconds.

EDITOR'S NOTE: This recipe was tested in a 1,100-watt microwave.

BACON 'N' EGG BURRITOS

BANANA COFFEE SMOOTHIE

BANANA COFFEE SMOOTHIE
YIELD: 1 SERVING

The banana and coffee pairing in this morning smoothie may seem a little different, but one sip of this creamy drink will convince you. It's perfect on busy mornings when you need to get out the door fast.

mia werner | madison, wisconsin

   3/4   cup 2% milk
   1/3   cup coffee yogurt
     1   small banana, frozen, peeled and cut into chunks
   1/8   teaspoon ground cinnamon
Dash ground nutmeg

In a blender, combine all ingredients; cover and process for 45-60 seconds or until blended. Pour into a chilled glass. Serve immediately.

EGGS TO GO
YIELD: 12 SERVINGS

These handy ham-and-cheese-packed egg "muffins" are the ultimate in kid-friendly fare. My children would always grab one of these on the way out the door to catch the bus.

christine smoot | childress, texas

     6   eggs, lightly beaten
     3   tablespoons butter, melted
  1-1/2   cups chopped deli ham
   1/2   cup dry bread crumbs
   1/4   cup shredded cheddar cheese
     1   tablespoon minced chives

In a large bowl, combine all ingredients. Fill greased muffin cups three-fourths full. Bake at 375° for 15-20 minutes or until a knife inserted near the center comes out clean. Serve eggs warm.

CHEESY EGG PUFFS
YIELD: 2-1/2 DOZEN

My father loves to entertain, and these buttery egg delights are one of his favorite items to serve at brunch. The leftovers are perfect for reheating in the microwave on busy mornings, so Dad always stashes a few aside for me to take home once the party is over.

amy soto | winfield, kansas

1/2	pound fresh mushrooms, sliced
4	green onions, chopped
1	tablespoon plus 1/2 cup butter, cubed, *divided*
1/2	cup all-purpose flour
1	teaspoon baking powder
1/2	teaspoon salt
10	eggs, lightly beaten
4	cups (16 ounces) shredded Monterey Jack cheese
2	cups (16 ounces) 4% cottage cheese

In a skillet, saute the mushrooms and onions in 1 tablespoon butter until tender. In a large bowl, combine the flour, baking powder and salt.

In another bowl, combine eggs and cheeses. Melt remaining butter; add to egg mixture. Stir into dry ingredients along with mushroom mixture.

Fill greased muffin cups three-fourths full. Bake at 350° for 35-40 minutes or until a knife inserted near the center comes out clean. Carefully run the knife around edge of muffin cups before removing.

CHEESY EGG PUFFS

BRUNCH POCKETS
YIELD: 4 SERVINGS

These hefty handfuls promise everyone a good, hot breakfast with little fuss. You'll love the toasty grab-and-go pockets stuffed with a delectable combination of pineapple, ham, turkey and cheese.

jean kimm | coeur d'alene, idaho

1	package (15 ounces) refrigerated pie crust
2	pineapple slices, cut in half
4	thin slices deli ham
4	thin slices deli turkey
4	slices Swiss cheese
1	egg, lightly beaten

Cut each pastry sheet into four wedges. Pat pineapple slices dry with paper towels. Top four pastry wedges with one slice each of ham, turkey, cheese and pineapple, folding meat and cheese to fit if necessary. Top each with a pastry wedge; seal and crimp edges with a fork. Cut slits in pastry.

Place on an ungreased baking sheet. Brush lightly with egg. Bake at 350° for 25-30 minutes or until golden brown. Serve pockets warm.

DAYBREAK SANDWICHES

DAYBREAK SANDWICHES
YIELD: 2 SERVINGS

Here's my family's healthy, homemade take on a fast-food favorite. My son-in-law created this recipe so my grandchildren could have a quick yet nutritious breakfast before school.

sharon pickett | aurora, indiana

2	eggs
1	teaspoon fat-free milk
1/4	teaspoon salt
1/8	teaspoon pepper
2	slices Canadian bacon (1/2 ounce *each*)
1	English muffin, split and toasted
2	tablespoons shredded reduced-fat cheddar cheese

In a small bowl, whisk the eggs, milk, salt and pepper. Divide between two 10-oz. microwave-safe custard cups coated with cooking spray. Microwave, uncovered, on high for 20 seconds. Stir; microwave 20-25 seconds longer or until center of egg is almost set.

Place a slice of bacon on each muffin half; top with egg and sprinkle with cheese. Microwave, uncovered, for 10-13 seconds or until cheese is melted. Let stand for 20-30 seconds before serving.

ANDOUILLE EGG BURRITOS

1 egg, lightly beaten
1-1/2 cups quick-cooking oats
1/2 cup sugar
1/2 cup milk
1/4 cup canola oil
1/4 cup chopped nuts
1/4 cups raisins
1 teaspoon baking powder
1/2 teaspoon salt
1/2 teaspoon ground cinnamon

Combine all ingredients in a large bowl. Pour mixture into a greased 8-in. square baking dish. Bake at 350° for 25 minutes. Let cool. Cut into squares.

ANDOUILLE EGG BURRITOS
YIELD: 6 SERVINGS

Give yourself a morning wake-up call with these spicy breakfast wraps. They make a great on-the-go breakfast, or try them weeknights for a delicious and different dinner.

frank millard | janesville, wisconsin

1/4 cup chopped onion
1 tablespoon butter
3/4 pound fully cooked andouille sausage links, sliced
1 tablespoon chopped green chilies
1 jalapeno pepper, seeded and chopped
8 eggs, lightly beaten
1/8 teaspoon salt
1/8 teaspoon pepper
Dash cayenne pepper
6 flour tortillas (8 inches), warmed
3 ounces pepper Jack cheese, shredded
Taco sauce, optional

In a large skillet over medium heat, cook onion in butter until tender. Add the sausage, chilies and jalapeno; cook 4-5 minutes longer or until heated through. Add the eggs, salt, pepper and cayenne; cook and stir until the eggs are completely set.

Spoon filling off center on each tortilla. Sprinkle each with 2 tablespoons cheese. Fold sides and ends over filling and roll up. Serve with taco sauce if desired.

> **EDITOR'S NOTE:** When cutting hot peppers, disposable gloves are recommended. Avoid touching your face.

BAKED OATMEAL SQUARES
YIELD: 4-6 SERVINGS

This quick and easy Amish breakfast bar recipe is one of my most cherished because it's hearty and flavorful. My husband loves the morning treats any time of day.

elaine heckman | bechtelsville, pennsylvania

CREAM CHEESE 'N' HAM BAGELS
YIELD: 2 SERVINGS

This is a speedy meal that's portable and satisfying. A chewy bagel is smothered with a flavorful cream cheese spread, then topped with Parmesan cheese and ham. Once the yummy bites are broiled to golden perfection, you'll agree it really hits the spot.

bill hilbrich | st. cloud, minnesota

2 plain bagels, split and toasted
2 garlic cloves, halved
2 ounces cream cheese, softened
1 cup finely chopped fully cooked ham
2 tablespoons shredded Parmesan cheese

Place bagels cut side up on an ungreased baking sheet; rub with cut sides of garlic. Spread with cream cheese. Top cream cheese with ham.

Broil 4 in. from the heat for 2-3 minutes or until heated through. Sprinkle with Parmesan cheese. Broil 1 minute longer or until cheese is slightly melted.

CREAM CHEESE 'N' HAM BAGELS

TOASTED ALMOND GRANOLA
YIELD: 8 CUPS

3	cups old-fashioned oats
2	cups crisp rice cereal
1/2	cup toasted wheat germ
1/2	cup nonfat dry milk powder
1/3	cup slivered almonds
1/4	cup packed brown sugar
2	tablespoons sunflower kernels
1/4	teaspoon salt
1/2	cup orange juice
1/4	cup honey
2	teaspoons canola oil
2	teaspoons vanilla extract
1/2	teaspoon almond extract
1	cup golden raisins
1	cup chopped dried apricots
1/2	cup dried cranberries

Fat-free plain yogurt, optional

In a large bowl, combine the oats, cereal, wheat germ, milk powder, almonds, sugar, sunflower kernels and salt. In a saucepan, combine the orange juice, honey and oil. Heat for 3-4 minutes over medium heat until honey is dissolved. Remove from the heat; stir in the extracts. Pour over the oat mixture; stir to coat.

Transfer to a 15-in. x 10-in. baking pan coated with cooking spray. Bake at 350° for 20-25 minutes or until crisp, stirring every 10 minutes. Remove and cool completely on a wire rack. Stir in dried fruits. Store in an airtight container. Serve with yogurt if desired.

TOASTED ALMOND GRANOLA

I combined several granola recipes to come up with this crunchy, cranberry-and-apricot treat. The possibilities are endless when you vary the kinds of dried fruits and nuts used in the mix.

tracy weakly | aloha, oregon

HAM 'N' EGG POCKETS
YIELD: 2 SERVINGS

1	egg
2	teaspoons milk
2	teaspoons butter
1	ounce thinly sliced deli ham, chopped
2	tablespoons shredded cheddar cheese
1	tube (4 ounces) refrigerated crescent rolls

In a small bowl, combine egg and milk. In a small skillet, heat butter until hot. Add egg mixture; cook and stir over medium heat until eggs are completely set. Remove from the heat. Fold in the ham and cheese.

On a greased baking sheet, separate crescent dough into two rectangles. Seal perforations; spoon half of the filling down the center of each rectangle. Fold in ends and sides; pinch to seal. Bake at 375° for 10-14 minutes or until golden brown.

HAM 'N' EGG POCKETS

Refrigerated crescent roll dough makes these savory bundles a snap to make in the morning. For a delicious variation, our home economists suggest substituting shredded Swiss cheese for the shredded cheddar cheese.

taste of home test kitchen

CORNMEAL WAFFLE SANDWICHES
YIELD: 6 SERVINGS

Craving a BLT for breakfast? Enjoy with this deliciously different morning version of the popular sandwich that features crisp bacon and fresh tomatoes layered between two golden cornmeal waffles. Prepare the waffles ahead of time and reheat in the toaster for quick assembly when time is short.

stacy joura | stoneboro, pennsylvania

3/4	cup all-purpose flour
3/4	cup cornmeal
1	tablespoon baking powder
1	tablespoon sugar
1	teaspoon salt
2	eggs, *separated*
1	cup milk
3	tablespoons butter, melted
1/2	cup shredded cheddar cheese

Mayonnaise

12	bacon strips, cooked and drained
2	small tomatoes, sliced

Salt and pepper to taste

In a large bowl, combine the first five ingredients. In another bowl, beat egg yolks. Add milk and butter; stir into dry ingredients just until moistened. Stir in cheese.

In a small bowl, beat egg whites until stiff peaks form; fold into the batter. Bake 12 waffles in a preheated waffle iron according to manufacturer's directions until golden brown. Spread mayonnaise on six waffles; top each with bacon, tomato, salt, pepper and remaining waffles. Serve immediately.

CORNMEAL WAFFLE SANDWICHES

CHOCOLATE BANANA SMOOTHIES
YIELD: 4 SERVINGS

These crowd-pleasing smoothies are a breeze to prepare and even easier to love. Get ready to make them over and over, because after one sip, they're going to be a hit!

renee zimmer | tacoma, washington

1	cup milk
1	cup vanilla yogurt
1/2	cup chocolate syrup
2	medium bananas, halved
8	ice cubes

In a blender, combine all ingredients; cover and process until smooth. Pour into chilled glasses; serve immediately.

BRUNCH EGG BURRITOS

BRUNCH EGG BURRITOS
YIELD: 4 SERVINGS

This recipe is a family favorite, and has been for many years. Besides being delicious, these burritos come together in no time!

jenny flake | gilbert, arizona

2	cups refrigerated shredded hash brown potatoes
3	tablespoons butter, *divided*
6	eggs
1/2	cup milk
1	can (4 ounces) chopped green chilies
1/4	teaspoon salt
1/4	teaspoon salt-free garlic seasoning blend
1/4	teaspoon pepper
4	to 6 drops Louisiana-style hot sauce
12	slices ready-to-serve fully cooked bacon, crumbled
2	cups (8 ounces) shredded Monterey Jack cheese
1	cup salsa
4	flour tortillas (10 inches), warmed

In a large skillet, cook potatoes in 2 tablespoons butter over medium heat for 6-7 minutes or until golden brown, stirring occasionally.

Meanwhile, in a small bowl, whisk the eggs, milk, chilies, seasonings and hot sauce. In another large skillet, heat remaining butter until hot. Add egg mixture; cook and stir over medium heat until eggs are completely set.

Layer 1/3 cup potatoes, about 1/2 cup egg mixture, 1/4 cup bacon, 1/2 cup cheese and 1/4 cup salsa off center on each tortilla. Fold sides and ends over filling and roll up. Serve immediately.

BACON 'N' EGG BAGELS
YIELD: 4 SERVINGS

Better than fast-food, these savory bites feature a veggie cream cheese and zesty olive spread that's topped with egg, bacon and cheese.

chris and jenny thackray | corpus christi, texas

- 4 bagels, split and toasted
- 1/2 cup garden vegetable cheese spread
- 1/2 cup sliced pimiento-stuffed olives
- 8 bacon strips, halved
- 4 eggs
- 4 slices Muenster cheese

Spread each bagel half with cheese spread. Place olives on bagel bottoms; set aside.

In a large skillet, cook bacon over medium heat until crisp. Using a slotted spoon, remove to paper towels; drain, reserving 3 tablespoons drippings.

Heat drippings over medium-hot heat. Add eggs; reduce heat to low. Fry until white is completely set and yolk begins to thicken but is not hard. Place an egg on each bagel bottom. Layer with cheese and bacon. Replace bagel tops.

BACON 'N' EGG BAGELS

BREAKFAST PARFAITS
YIELD: 4 SERVINGS

With pineapples, raspberries and bananas, these yogurt treats are a snappy breakfast choice when you're in a hurry.

adell meyer | madison, wisconsin

- 2 cups pineapple chunks
- 1 cup fresh *or* frozen raspberries
- 1 cup (8 ounces) vanilla yogurt
- 1 cup sliced ripe banana
- 1/2 cup chopped dates *or* raisins
- 1/4 cup sliced almonds

In four parfait glasses or serving dishes, layer the pineapple, raspberries, yogurt, banana and dates. Sprinkle with almonds. Serve immediately.

ORANGE PEACH SMOOTHIES

ORANGE PEACH SMOOTHIES
YIELD: 4 SERVINGS

This eye-opening shake is wonderful on summer mornings. I make the smoothies often when peaches are in season, but canned or frozen peaches work just as well. Everyone is surprised to discover almond extract is the mystery ingredient.

kara cook | elk ridge, utah

- 2 cups frozen unsweetened peach slices, thawed
- 1 cup milk
- 1 can (6 ounces) frozen orange juice concentrate, thawed
- 1/4 teaspoon almond extract
- 1 pint vanilla ice cream
- 3 drops *each* red and yellow food coloring, optional

In a blender, combine the peaches, milk, orange juice concentrate and almond extract.

Add ice cream; cover and process until smooth. Add the red and yellow food coloring if desired. Pour smoothies into chilled glasses; serve immediately.

Breakfast TIP

Adding cottage cheese to smoothies makes them extra thick and creamy. Plus it adds an extra measure of protein and calcium for my children, which makes me feel even better about serving them as a quick breakfast or nutritious snacks.

—Michele M., Henniker, New Hampshire

HAZELNUT MOCHA SMOOTHIES
YIELD: 3 SERVINGS

Coffee lovers will rejoice after one taste of this decadent morning smoothie created by our home economists. They think you'll agree that this rich sipper is just as good as any coffee-shop version.

taste of home test kitchen

1	cup milk
1/2	cup chocolate hazelnut spread
4	teaspoons instant espresso powder
6	ice cubes
2	cups vanilla ice cream

Chocolate curls, optional

In a blender, combine the milk, hazelnut spread and espresso powder; cover and process until blended. Add ice cubes; cover and process until smooth. Add ice cream; cover and process until smooth. Pour into chilled glasses; serve immediately. Garnish with chocolate curls if desired.

EDITOR'S NOTE: Look for chocolate hazelnut spread in the peanut butter section.

HAZELNUT MOCHA SMOOTHIES

OATMEAL BREAKFAST BARS
YIELD: ABOUT 2-1/2 DOZEN

These soft and chewy bars have a hint of orange marmalade, giving them a flavor that's a fun change of pace from typical granola bars. They're so easy to whip up and so delicious, you'll find yourself making them whenever you can.

barbara nowakowski | north tonawanda, new york

4	cups quick-cooking oats
1	cup packed brown sugar
1	teaspoon salt
1-1/2	cups chopped walnuts
1	cup flaked coconut
3/4	cup butter, melted
3/4	cup orange marmalade

In a large bowl, combine the oats, brown sugar and salt. Stir in remaining ingredients. Press into a greased 15-in. x 10-in. baking pan. Bake at 425° for 15-17 minutes or until golden brown. Cool on a wire rack.

STUFFED BREAKFAST BURRITOS
YIELD: 2 SERVINGS

Soon after my family moved to Arizona, I received this recipe. It's a big hit with everyone. For a nice variation, add part of a green pepper and some whole kernel corn. Or, omit the potatoes and eggs and add your favorite canned beans and a little shredded cheddar cheese.

anita meador | mesa, arizona

1/4	pound bulk pork sausage
1/2	cup cooked diced peeled potatoes
2	tablespoons chopped onion
4	teaspoons canned chopped green chilies

Dash pepper

2	eggs, lightly beaten
1/2	cup shredded taco cheese
2	flour tortillas (8 inches), warmed

Crumble sausage into a skillet; cook over medium heat until no longer pink. Remove sausage with a slotted spoon and set aside.

In the same skillet, fry potatoes and onion until onion is crisp-tender. Add the chilies and pepper. Return sausage to the pan. Add eggs; cook and stir until eggs are completely set.

Remove from the heat; stir in cheese. Spoon mixture off-center onto tortillas. Fold in bottom and sides of tortilla and roll up.

Breakfast TIP

Most bars, such as Oatmeal Breakfast Bars, will freeze well for up to 3 months. To freeze a pan of uncut bars, place them in an airtight container or resealable plastic bag. Or for an easy on-the-go bite, wrap individual bars in plastic wrap and stack them in an airtight container. Simply remove from the freezer the night before and thaw at room temperature.

SAUSAGE OMELET BAGELS

SAUSAGE OMELET BAGELS
YIELD: 2 SERVINGS

What a great way to start the day! These spicy breakfast sandwiches are hearty enough to take you through a busy morning. They can even double as a speedy supper.

cindie haras | boca raton, florida

2	tablespoons mayonnaise
1	teaspoon lime juice
1	teaspoon minced fresh cilantro
3	eggs
1	teaspoon finely chopped jalapeno pepper
1/4	teaspoon salt
1/8	teaspoon pepper
4	breakfast turkey sausage links
1	slice (1 ounce) pepper Jack cheese
2	plain bagels (4 inches *each*), split

Dash chili powder

2	teaspoons salsa
2	slices red onion

In a small bowl, combine the mayonnaise, lime juice and cilantro; set aside. In another bowl, whisk the eggs, jalapeno, salt and pepper; set aside.

In a small nonstick skillet, cook sausage over medium heat for 10-12 minutes or until no longer pink; drain. Remove and keep warm. Pour egg mixture into the skillet; cook over medium heat. As eggs set, lift edges, letting uncooked portion flow underneath. When the eggs are set, place cheese over one side; fold omelet over cheese. Cover; stand for 1-1/2 minutes or until the cheese is melted.

Cut omelet in half; place on bagel bottoms. Cut sausage links in half lengthwise; place over omelets. Sprinkle with chili powder. Top with salsa and onion. Spread cut side of bagel tops with mayonnaise mixture; place over onion. Broil 6 in. from the heat for 2-3 minutes or until heated through. Serve sandwiches immediately.

EDITOR'S NOTE: When cutting hot peppers, disposable gloves are recommended. Avoid touching your face.

BANANA BREAKFAST SMOOTHIES
YIELD: 2 SERVINGS

Enjoy a fast and nutritious breakfast drink with this refreshing and healthful blend of yogurt, wheat germ and bananas. Try pairing the creamy beverage with a muffin or a piece of toast in the morning.

stacy myers | bristol, tennessee

1	cup fat-free milk
1/2	cup fat-free plain yogurt
1/4	cup toasted wheat germ
2	small ripe bananas, sliced and frozen
1	teaspoon sugar
1	teaspoon vanilla extract

Ground nutmeg

Place the first six ingredients in a blender; cover and process for 1-2 minutes or until smooth. Pour into chilled glasses; sprinkle with nutmeg. Serve immediately.

GRANOLA CEREAL BARS
YIELD: 1 DOZEN

These sweet, peanut butter-flavored granola bars are perfect for breakfast, dessert or even a quick snack.

helen velichko | kansas city, missouri

1/2	cup packed brown sugar
1/2	cup creamy peanut butter
1/4	cup light corn syrup
1	teaspoon vanilla extract
2	cups old-fashioned oats
1-1/2	cups crisp rice cereal
1/4	cup miniature chocolate chips

In a microwave-safe bowl, combine the brown sugar, peanut butter and corn syrup; cover and microwave on high for 2 minutes or until mixture comes to a boil, stirring once. Stir in the vanilla extract; add oats and cereal. Fold in chocolate chips. Press into a 9-in. square pan coated with cooking spray. Let cool; cut into bars.

GRANOLA CEREAL BARS

SPICY SCRAMBLED EGG SANDWICHES

SPICY SCRAMBLED EGG SANDWICHES
YIELD: 4 SERVINGS

My family adores these zesty, filling morning bites. Sandwiched between toasted English muffins, the fluffy scrambled eggs are packed with veggies, flavor and nutrition!

helen vail | glenside, pennsylvania

1/3	cup chopped green pepper
1/4	cup chopped onion
3	eggs
4	egg whites
1	tablespoon water
1/4	teaspoon salt
1/4	teaspoon ground mustard
1/8	teaspoon pepper
1/8	teaspoon hot pepper sauce
1/3	cup fresh *or* frozen corn, thawed
1/4	cup real bacon bits
4	English muffins, split and toasted

In a 10-in. skillet coated with cooking spray, cook chopped green pepper and onion over medium heat until vegetables are tender, about 8 minutes.

In a large bowl, whisk the eggs, egg whites, water, salt, mustard, pepper and hot pepper sauce. Pour into skillet. Add corn and bacon; cook and stir until the eggs are completely set. Spoon onto English muffin bottoms; replace tops. Serve sandwiches immediately.

BREAKFAST PUFFS
YIELD: 2 DOZEN

Getting kids to eat breakfast is a breeze when you offer them these little bundles of goodness packed with hearty ingredients. Kids think it's like eating a savory breakfast cookie!

bernice williams | north aurora, illinois

1/2	cup butter, softened
2	tablespoons orange juice concentrate
1	egg, lightly beaten
1-1/2	cups all-purpose flour
2/3	cup sugar
1/2	cup Grape-Nuts cereal
1	teaspoon baking powder
1/2	pound sliced bacon, cooked and crumbled

In a bowl, beat butter and orange juice. Add egg; mix well. Combine flour, sugar, cereal and baking powder; stir into butter mixture. Fold in bacon.

Drop by rounded teaspoonfuls onto ungreased baking sheets. Bake at 350° for 11-13 minutes or until edges are lightly brown. Store in the refrigerator.

PEACHY FRUIT SMOOTHIES
YIELD: 6 SERVINGS

The color of this fruity sipper just says "refreshment!" Our home economists who created this tantalizing beverage agree it is great for breakfast, dessert or as a midday pick-me-up.

taste of home test kitchen

1-1/4	cups milk
1	cup (8 ounces) lemon yogurt
1	cup orange juice
3	tablespoons sugar
1/2	teaspoon vanilla extract
1	package (16 ounces) frozen unsweetened peach slices

In a blender, combine all the ingredients; cover and process until smooth. Serve in chilled glasses.

PEACHY FRUIT SMOOTHIES

MORNING WRAPS

MORNING WRAPS
YIELD: 4 SERVINGS

We like quick and simple morning meals during the week, and these wraps fill the bill because I can prepare them ahead of time. With just a minute in the microwave, breakfast is ready.

betty kleberger | florissant, missouri

6	eggs
2	tablespoons milk
1/4	teaspoon pepper
1	tablespoon canola oil
1	cup (4 ounces) shredded cheddar cheese
3/4	cup diced fully cooked ham
4	flour tortillas (8 inches), warmed

In a small bowl, whisk the eggs, milk and pepper. In a large skillet, heat oil. Add egg mixture; cook and stir over medium heat until eggs are completely set. Stir in cheese and ham.

Spoon egg mixture down the center of each tortilla; roll up. Serve immediately, or wrap in plastic wrap and freeze in a resealable plastic bag.

To use frozen wraps: Thaw in the refrigerator overnight. Remove plastic wrap; wrap tortilla in a moist microwave-safe paper towel. Microwave on high for 30-60 seconds or until heated through. Serve immediately.

NUT 'N' FRUIT GRANOLA
YIELD: 9 CUPS

After a friend brought this crunchy, fruit-filled treat on a camping trip, I requested the recipe and lightened it up. The munchable medley is fantastic on its own, but I also suggest trying it over low-fat vanilla yogurt or with a splash of milk.

rachel dandeneau | dummer, new hampshire

4	cups old-fashioned oats
1	cup flaked coconut
1/2	cup toasted wheat germ
1/2	cup slivered almonds
1/4	cup unsalted sunflower kernels
1/2	cup honey
1/4	cup orange juice
2	tablespoons canola oil
1-1/2	teaspoons ground cinnamon
1/4	teaspoon salt
1	teaspoon vanilla extract
1	cup dried mixed fruit
1	cup raisins
1/2	cup dried cranberries

Milk, optional

In a large bowl, combine the first five ingredients and set aside. In a small saucepan, combine the honey, orange juice, oil, cinnamon and salt; cook and stir over medium heat for 3 minutes. Remove from the heat; stir in vanilla extract. Pour over oat mixture; stir to coat.

Transfer to a 15-in. x 10-in. baking pan coated with cooking spray. Bake at 350° for 25-30 minutes or until golden brown, stirring 3-4 times. Cool on a wire rack.

Place oat mixture in a large bowl. Stir in the dried fruit, raisins and cranberries. Store in an airtight container in a cool dry place for up to 2 months. Serve with milk if desired.

MANGO BANANA SMOOTHIES
YIELD: 2 SERVINGS

Toasted wheat germ is a healthy bonus in this tropical treasure. The chilly orange and mango flavors really shine through in this creamy beverage that's ideal for busy mornings.

verna puntigan | spartanburg, south carolina

1/2	cup orange juice
1/2	cup vanilla yogurt
1	cup chopped peeled mango
1	medium ripe banana, sliced and frozen
2	tablespoons honey
2	teaspoons toasted wheat germ
1	teaspoon candied ginger

Place all ingredients in a blender; cover and process for 1-2 minutes or until smooth. Pour into chilled glasses; serve immediately.

KIDS' WEEKEND FAVORITES

SLEEPING IN LATE...SATURDAY CARTOONS...NOW THERE'S MORE TO LOVE ABOUT THE WEEKEND THANKS TO THIS YUMMY BREAKFAST FARE.

**FRUITY FRENCH
TOAST SANDWICHES
PAGE 73**

PEANUT BUTTER HONEYBEES

Children of all ages find these cute, little snacks irresistible. Even the youngest "chefs" can help out in the kitchen by crunching the graham crackers or by measuring and mixing the ingredients.

heather bazinet | ingleside, ontario

PEANUT BUTTER HONEYBEES
YIELD: 4 DOZEN

1/2	cup creamy peanut butter
2	tablespoons butter, softened
1/2	cup confectioners' sugar
3/4	cup graham cracker crumbs
1	square (1 ounce) semisweet chocolate
1/3	cup sliced almonds, toasted

In a small bowl, cream the peanut butter, butter and confectioners' sugar until smooth. Stir in crumbs.

Shape a teaspoonful of dough into 1-1/2-in. ovals; place on a waxed paper-lined baking sheet. Place chocolate in a small microwave-safe bowl; microwave on high for 1 minute or until melted. Let stand for 5 minutes.

Transfer melted chocolate to a resealable plastic bag; cut a very small hole in corner in bag. Pipe three stripes on each bee. Insert two almonds into each bee for wings. Use a toothpick to poke holes for eyes. Store the treats in the refrigerator.

In a large bowl, beat eggs. Add milk, vanilla, cinnamon and nutmeg. Add bread cubes and toss; let stand for 5 minutes. Melt butter in a large skillet. Add bread cubes and stir until cooked and browned. Gradually add the sugar; stir to coat evenly. Cook until all sugar is dissolved, about 5 minutes.

SUMMER MELON PARFAITS

SUMMER MELON PARFAITS
YIELD: 4 SERVINGS

Picky eaters who don't care for fruit will gobble up this treat whipped up by our home economists that features yogurt and frozen whipped topping. It will refresh you and your family in the heat of summer, no matter what time of day it's offered.

taste of home test kitchen

1/4	cup thawed lemonade concentrate
1/4	cup lemon, orange *or* raspberry yogurt
1	carton (8 ounces) frozen whipped topping, thawed
1	cup diced honeydew
1	cup diced cantaloupe

In a large bowl, combine lemonade concentrate and yogurt; fold in whipped topping. In each of four dessert glasses, layer with 1/4 cup honeydew, 1/4 cup lemon mixture, 1/4 cup cantaloupe and remaining lemon mixture.

SCRAMBLED FRENCH TOAST
YIELD: 6-8 SERVINGS

I make a point of saving my leftover bread just so I can make this family-favorite recipe. Little ones will have fun helping you prepare it, but are sure to enjoy eating this sticky "scrambled" version of French toast even more!

torrey stuart | eugene, oregon

4	eggs
2	cups milk
2	teaspoons vanilla extract
1	teaspoon ground cinnamon
1/2	teaspoon ground nutmeg
12	cups cubed day-old bread (1/2-inch cubes)
3	tablespoons butter
1/2	to 2/3 cup sugar

WAGON WHEEL BREAKFAST PIE
YIELD: 2 SERVINGS

This cute eye-opener is loaded with flavor. The recipe originally came from a military magazine. I've prepared it several times, and it's been quite popular, especially with children of all ages.

sandra hough | hampton, virginia

1-1/2	cups frozen shredded hash brown potatoes, thawed
3	tablespoons cream cheese, softened
2	tablespoons plus 2 teaspoons 2% milk, *divided*
1	green onion, chopped
1/8	teaspoon salt, optional
Dash pepper	
4	uncooked breakfast sausage links
1/4	cup biscuit/baking mix
1	egg
Dash ground nutmeg	
Dash paprika	

Place the hash browns in a 7-in. pie plate coated with cooking spray. In a small bowl, combine the cream cheese, 2 tablespoons milk, onion, salt if desired and pepper; spread over the hash browns.

Cut the sausage links in half lengthwise; arrange the cut sausage links over the hash browns in a spoke-like fashion.

In a small bowl, whisk the biscuit mix, egg, nutmeg and remaining milk until smooth; pour between sausages. Sprinkle with paprika. Bake at 400° for 25-30 minutes or until golden brown and the filling is bubbly.

WAGON WHEEL BREAKFAST PIE

SNACK BARS
YIELD: 5 DOZEN

If your family likes granola bars, they're sure to love these tempting treats. Full of hearty ingredients, they're a perfect snack for taking along on picnics and road trips or for packing in brown-bag lunches.

carolyn fisher | kinzer, pennsylvania

- 9 cups Rice Chex, crushed
- 6 cups quick-cooking oats
- 1 cup graham cracker crumbs
- 1 cup flaked coconut
- 1/2 cup toasted wheat germ
- 2 packages (one 16 ounces, one 10-1/2 ounces) large marshmallows
- 1 cup butter, cubed
- 1/2 cup honey
- 1-1/2 cups raisins, M&M's miniature baking bits *or* miniature semisweet chocolate chips, optional

In a very large bowl, combine the first five ingredients. In a Dutch oven over low heat, cook and stir marshmallows and butter until the marshmallows are melted. Add honey and mix well.

Pour over cereal mixture; stir until blended. Add the raisins, M&M's or chocolate chips if desired. Pat two-thirds into a greased 15-in. x 10-in. pan and the remaining third into a 9-in. square pan. Cool before cutting into bars.

MONKEY BREAD
YIELD: 10-12 SERVINGS

Both of my boys really had a blast helping me make Monkey Bread when they were young. It always seemed to taste twice as good when they helped fix it.

carol allen | mcleansboro, illinois

- 1 package (3-1/2 ounces) cook-and-serve butterscotch pudding mix
- 3/4 cup sugar
- 3 teaspoons ground cinnamon
- 1/2 cup finely chopped pecans, optional
- 1/2 cup butter, melted
- 3 tubes (10 ounces *each*) refrigerated biscuits

In a large resealable plastic bag, combine the pudding mix, sugar, cinnamon and pecans if desired. Pour the butter into a shallow bowl. Cut the biscuits into quarters. Dip several pieces into the butter, then place in bag and shake to coat.

Arrange in a greased 10-in. fluted tube pan. Repeat until all the biscuit pieces are coated. Bake at 350° for 30-35 minutes or until browned. Cool bread for 30 minutes before inverting onto a serving plate.

PEANUT BUTTER 'N' JELLY BREAKFAST SHAKE
YIELD: 2 SERVINGS (2-1/2 CUPS)

My husband is a big kid at heart, who will often whip up this tasty shake for an on-the-go breakfast. Your kids will love the peanut butter and jelly sandwich flavor blended into it.

loretta levitz | allston, massachusetts

- 2 cups cold milk
- 1 ripe banana, sliced
- 2 tablespoons peanut butter
- 2 tablespoons jam, jelly *or* preserves (any flavor)
- 1/2 teaspoon vanilla extract

In a blender, place all ingredients; cover and process for 3 minutes or until mixture is smooth. Pour shake into chilled glasses; serve immediately.

VOLCANO PANCAKE
YIELD: 8 SERVINGS

Our daughter, Charity, enjoys making this cheesy puff pancake, then peeking in the oven to see how high it's risen. For a sweet version, you can eliminate the shredded cheddar cheese and serve it with confectioners' sugar or maple syrup instead.

kay curtis | guthrie, oklahoma

6	eggs
1	cup milk
1	cup all-purpose flour
1/2	teaspoon salt
1/2	cup butter, melted
3/4	cup shredded cheddar cheese

In a bowl, beat the eggs. Add milk, flour and salt; stir until smooth. Pour butter into a 13-in. x 9-in. baking pan. Add batter.

Bake at 400° for 30-35 minutes or until a knife inserted near the center comes out clean. Sprinkle pancake with shredded cheddar cheese. Serve immediately.

SPRINKLE FRUIT DIP
YIELD: 3 CUPS

Making this creamy mixture especially festive are its bright candy sprinkles. Served with an assortment of fresh fruit "dippers," it's a fun addition to a slumber party breakfast.

leslie miller | butler, pennsylvania

1-1/2	cups strawberry yogurt
1-1/2	cups whipped topping
1/4	cup colored sprinkles, *divided*
4	large green apples, sliced
4	large red apples, sliced
2	pints fresh strawberries
4	cups red *and/or* green grapes

In a bowl, fold together yogurt, whipped topping and half of the sprinkles. Cover and refrigerate for 20 minutes. Just before serving, top with remaining sprinkles. Serve with fruit.

SPRINKLE FRUIT DIP

BUNNY PINEAPPLE SMOOTHIES

BUNNY PINEAPPLE SMOOTHIES
YIELD: 10 SERVINGS

After trying these bunny-topped smoothies created by our home economists, you'll want to hop back to the buffet for extra servings. Flavored with orange juice, pineapple sherbet and pina colada yogurt, they add a tropical taste to morning meals.

taste of home test kitchen

2	cups orange juice
2	pints pineapple sherbet
4	cartons (8 ounces *each*) pina colada yogurt
4	medium bananas, quartered
1	cup milk
1	teaspoon vanilla extract
2	cups whipped topping, *divided*
1	drop red food coloring

In a blender, combine half of the orange juice, sherbet, yogurt, bananas, milk and vanilla; cover and process until smooth. Pour into chilled glasses. Repeat.

Place 1-1/2 cups whipped topping in a pastry or plastic bag; cut a medium hole in a corner of the bag. Pipe a bunny face on each smoothie.

Tint remaining whipped topping with food coloring; place in another bag. Cut a small hole in a corner of the bag. Pipe eyes, nose and inside of ears on each bunny face. Beginning from the nose, gently pull a toothpick through the whipped topping toward the edge of the glass to form whiskers. Serve immediately.

FRUITY FRENCH TOAST SANDWICHES
YIELD: 2 SERVINGS

4	fresh strawberries, sliced
1/2	medium firm banana, sliced
4	slices French bread (3/4 inch thick)
1	egg
2	tablespoons half-and-half cream
1/4	teaspoon ground cinnamon
1/4	teaspoon vanilla extract
1	teaspoon canola oil
1	teaspoon confectioners' sugar

In a bowl, combine strawberry and banana slices. Place 1/4 cup on two slices of bread, arranging fruit in a single layer; top with remaining bread. Set remaining fruit aside.

In a shallow bowl, beat the egg, cream, cinnamon and vanilla. Dip both sides of sandwiches into egg mixture. Heat oil on a griddle; cook French toast for 3-4 minutes on each side or until golden brown. Sprinkle with confectioners' sugar. Serve with reserved fruit.

FRUITY FRENCH TOAST SANDWICHES

These pretty breakfast sandwiches are quick, effortless and taste like they came straight from a French kitchen. The delightful morning bites, which can easily be doubled for guests, are also a great way to use up leftover French bread.

jessica walston | granbury, texas

PUPPY DOG PANCAKES

The too-cute puppy dog appearance of these yummy pancakes will win kids over instantly. Our home economists suggest having children help assemble and decorate the puppy faces.

taste of home test kitchen

PUPPY DOG PANCAKES
YIELD: 4 PUPPY DOG PANCAKES

1	cup all-purpose flour
1	teaspoon sugar
3/4	teaspoon baking powder
1/2	teaspoon salt
1	egg
1	cup buttermilk
1	tablespoon butter, melted
1	tablespoon chocolate syrup
2	drops strawberry syrup
8	semisweet chocolate chips

In a large bowl, combine the flour, sugar, baking powder and salt. In another large bowl, whisk the egg, buttermilk and butter. Stir into the dry ingredients just until moistened. Place 2/3 cup of batter in a small bowl; stir in chocolate syrup. Place 1 teaspoon of batter in another bowl; stir in strawberry syrup.

For puppy ears, pour eight 1 tablespoonfuls of chocolate batter onto a lightly greased large hot griddle. For muzzle and eyes, spoon eight 1 teaspoonfuls and eight 1/4 teaspoonfuls of chocolate batter onto the griddle. For tongues, spoon four 1/8 teaspoonfuls of pink batter onto the griddle. Turn when bubbles form on top of pancakes; cook until the second side is golden brown.

To assemble, arrange ears, eyes, muzzle and tongue on plain pancakes; top eyes with chocolate chips.

FUNNY FACE TOAST

FUNNY FACE TOAST
YIELD: 1 SERVING

My two young boys are enthusiastic about learning to cook. So whenever I head for the kitchen, they volunteer to measure, scoop, pour and stir. And with this fun breakfast idea, they also practice their "painting"...without ruining my walls!

mary kay morris | cokato, minnesota

    1   tablespoon milk for *each* color desired
    3   to 4 drops food coloring of any colors desired
Bread

In a small bowl, combine milk and food coloring. With a small spoon, cotton swabs or clean small paintbrush, "paint" a face on a piece of bread. Toast.

BREAKFAST RICE PUDDING
YIELD: 8 SERVINGS

My husband makes this rice pudding quite often for our breakfast. It's cozy and comforting fare on cold winter mornings.

sue draheim | waterford, wisconsin

1-1/3   cups uncooked long grain *or* basmati rice
    1   can (15-1/4 ounces) peach halves, drained
    1   cup canned *or* frozen pitted tart cherries, drained
    1   cup heavy whipping cream
  1/2   cup packed brown sugar, *divided*
  1/4   cup old-fashioned oats
  1/4   cup flaked coconut
  1/4   cup chopped pecans
  1/4   cup butter, melted

Cook rice according to package directions. In a large bowl, combine the rice, peaches, cherries, cream and 1/4 cup brown sugar. Transfer to a greased 1-1/2-quart baking dish.

Combine the oats, coconut, pecans, butter and remaining brown sugar; sprinkle over rice. Bake, uncovered, at 375° for 25-30 minutes or until golden brown.

EDITOR'S NOTE: This recipe is equally good with fresh blueberries instead of the cherries.

FLOWER WITH BUTTERFLIES
YIELD: 1 FRUIT PLATE

It's easy to inspire kids to gobble up their fruit with this fun, eye-catching treat. They may even want to help create the pretty garden scene on their plate.

shirley piepenburg | boyne city, michigan

    1   medium honeydew melon
    2   red apple slices
    2   large fresh strawberries
Fresh mint, optional
    2   navel orange slices (1/4 inch thick), halved

Cut melon in half lengthwise (from top to bottom), cut three 1/4-in.-thick slices from one half. Remove and discard rind and seeds; set slices aside for flower stem and leaves. Cover and refrigerate remaining melon for another use.

For flower, place apple slices, peel side out, at the top of a large plate. Cut one strawberry into four slices; arrange on top of apples. Cut second berry into quarters; set aside for butterflies. Trim one melon slice to 1/2-in. width; position under flower for stem. Cut remaining melon slices into leaf shapes; place next to stem. Add the fresh mint for additional leaves if desired.

Arrange butterflies on either side of flower. Place two orange slice halves, peel side together, to form wings. Place a strawberry quarter in the center of each set of wings for butterfly body (use remaining strawberry pieces of another use).

FLOWER WITH BUTTERFLIES

FOUR-FOOD-GROUP SHAKES

FOUR-FOOD-GROUP SHAKES
YIELD: 2 SERVINGS

We created this thick peanut butter and banana shake while teaching our 5-year-old son about the four basic food groups. It's a quick and delicious breakfast or snack that he enjoys making for family and friends.

heather fortney | gahanna, ohio

1/2　cup milk
　1　cup vanilla ice cream, softened
　1　medium ripe banana, cut into chunks
　1　whole graham cracker, broken into large pieces
　2　tablespoons peanut butter
　2　tablespoons chocolate syrup
Cinnamon-sugar, optional

In a blender, combine the first six ingredients; cover and process until smooth. Pour into chilled glasses; sprinkle with cinnamon-sugar if desired. Serve immediately.

KIDS' CREPE ROLL-UPS
YIELD: 5 SERVINGS

Your kiddos will enjoy popping these little crepe bites into their mouths. But watch out! Whenever I prepare a batch of them for my hungry bunch, they disappear quickly.

phyllis grodahl | lytton, iowa

1-1/2　cups milk
　2　eggs
　1　cup all-purpose flour

1/2　teaspoon salt
　1　tablespoon butter, melted
Maple syrup

In a blender, combine the milk, eggs, flour and salt. Cover and process until smooth. Heat a lightly greased nonstick 6-in. skillet. Add 1/4 cup of batter. Lift and tilt pan to evenly coat bottom.

Cook on each side until golden. Repeat with remaining batter. Roll up and slice into bite-size pieces. Drizzle with butter and syrup.

JAM 'N' CREAM FRENCH TOAST
YIELD: 1 SERVING

My grandmother used to make this sweet, special version of French toast for me when I was a child. Feel free to experiment with other flavors of jam and bread, as well.

b. mackinnon | kodak, tennessee

　2　tablespoons cream cheese, softened
　2　thick slices cinnamon-raisin bread
　2　tablespoons strawberry jam
　1　egg
　1　tablespoon butter
Maple syrup, optional

Spread cream cheese on one slice of bread. Spread jam on the other slice; place jam side down over the cream cheese. In a shallow bowl, beat egg. Dip both sides of bread into egg.

In a skillet, melt butter; cook bread for 3-4 minutes on each side or until golden brown. Serve with syrup if desired.

JAM 'N' CREAM FRENCH TOAST

MANDARIN ORANGE BREAKFAST BITES
YIELD: 2-1/2 DOZEN

These yummy, orange-flavored nibbles taste like doughnuts without the hassle of rolling out dough and frying. Our daughter likes me to have them waiting for her and her friends after school.

delores thompson | clear lake, iowa

1-1/2   cups all-purpose flour
1/2   cup sugar
1-3/4   teaspoons baking powder
1/2   teaspoon salt
1/2   teaspoon ground nutmeg
1/2   cup butter, softened
1   egg
1/2   cup milk
1   teaspoon almond extract
1   can (11 ounces) mandarin oranges, drained and diced

TOPPING:

1/3   cup sugar
1   teaspoon ground cinnamon
1/2   cup butter, melted

In a large bowl, combine the first five ingredients. Cut in butter until mixture resembles coarse crumbs. In another bowl, whisk the egg, milk and extract. Stir into crumb mixture just until moistened. Fold in oranges.

Fill greased or paper-lined miniature muffin cups two-thirds full. Bake at 350° for 15-20 minutes. Cool for 5 minutes before removing from pans to wire racks. Combine sugar and cinnamon. Dip tops of warm muffins in melted butter, then in cinnamon-sugar.

JAZZED-UP FRENCH TOAST STICKS
YIELD: 3 SERVINGS

Store-bought French toast sticks are spread with strawberry cream cheese to make this indulgent breakfast fare. I often serve the "stuffed" French toast with a citrusy fruit puree instead of syrup.

anna free | bradner, ohio

4   ounces spreadable strawberry cream cheese
12   French toast sticks
1   snack-size cup (4 ounces) mixed fruit
1   tablespoon orange juice
Sliced fresh strawberries, optional

Spread cream cheese over six French toast sticks, about 1 tablespoon on each; top with remaining sticks. Place in a greased 9-in. square baking pan. Bake at 400° for 15-17 minutes or until golden brown.

Meanwhile, in a blender, combine mixed fruit and orange juice; cover and process until smooth. Serve with French toast sticks. Garnish with strawberries if desired.

BUTTERFLY PANCAKES

BUTTERFLY PANCAKES
YIELD: 5 BUTTERFLY PANCAKES

Who says you can't play with your food? Our home economists created these fun pancakes that are shaped like butterflies, making breakfast an extra-special treat.

taste of home test kitchen

1   cup all-purpose flour
1   teaspoon sugar
3/4   teaspoon baking powder
1/2   teaspoon salt
1   egg
1   cup buttermilk
1   tablespoon butter, melted
Assorted fresh fruit

In a large bowl, combine the flour, sugar, baking powder and salt. In another bowl, whisk the egg, buttermilk and butter. Stir into the dry ingredients just until moistened.

To form each butterfly wing, pour 2 tablespoons of batter onto a lightly greased hot griddle. Pour 1 tablespoon of batter below and touching the larger one. Turn when bubbles form on top of pancakes; cook until second side is golden brown.

To assemble, place two wings on a serving plate, forming a butterfly. Top with fruit.

Breakfast TIP

Make your own French toast sticks using leftover hot dog buns. Split each in half before dipping in the egg batter. My kids loved them!

—Leigh D., South Hadley, Massachusetts

BUTTERSCOTCH TOAST

YIELD: 6-8 SERVINGS

I first started using this recipe decades ago when my children were little. They were always delighted when this showed up on the Saturday morning breakfast table. And I was delighted that they were taking the time to sit and eat breakfast!

gerry rice | greenville, michigan

1/4	cup packed brown sugar
3	tablespoons butter, softened
1	teaspoon half-and-half cream
6	to 8 pieces of toast

In a bowl, beat brown sugar, butter and cream until smooth. Spread on toast. Broil toast 4 in. from the heat for 1-2 minutes or until bubbly.

BREAKFAST BANANA SPLITS

YIELD: 2 SERVINGS

I can't brag enough about this recipe. It's eye-fetching enough for a formal brunch, yet easy to prepare for everyday enjoyment. With different fruits and cereals, the variations are endless.

renee lloyd | pearl, mississippi

1	medium firm banana
1/3	cup *each* blueberries, halved seedless grapes, sliced kiwifruit and strawberries
1	cup vanilla yogurt
1/2	cup granola cereal with almonds
2	maraschino cherries with stems

Slice banana in half lengthwise; cut each in half widthwise. Place two pieces of banana in two individual bowls. Top each with 2/3 cup mixed fruit, 1/2 cup vanilla yogurt, 1/4 cup granola and 1 maraschino cherry.

BREAKFAST BANANA SPLITS

BREAKFAST PIZZA

BREAKFAST PIZZA

YIELD: 6 SLICES

Who wouldn't scramble to the table when you tell them you're serving pizza for breakfast! My family requests this potato, egg and cheese topped pie often for breakfast—or even dinner.

christy hinrichs | parkville, missouri

2	cups frozen shredded hash brown potatoes
1/4	teaspoon ground cumin
1/4	teaspoon chili powder
2	tablespoons canola oil, *divided*
4	eggs
2	tablespoons milk
1/4	teaspoon salt
2	green onions, chopped
2	tablespoons diced sweet red pepper
1	tablespoon finely chopped jalapeno pepper
1	garlic clove, minced
1	prebaked thin Italian bread shell crust (16 ounces)
1/2	cup salsa
3/4	cup shredded cheddar cheese

In a large nonstick skillet, cook the hash browns, cumin and chili powder in 1 tablespoon oil over medium heat until golden. Remove and keep warm.

In a small bowl, beat the eggs, milk and salt; set aside. In the same skillet, saute the onions, peppers and garlic in remaining oil until tender. Add egg mixture. Cook and stir over medium heat until almost set. Remove from the heat.

Place crust on an ungreased 14-in. pizza pan. Spread salsa over crust. Top with egg mixture. Sprinkle with hash browns and cheese. Bake at 375° for 8-10 minutes or until cheese is melted.

EDITOR'S NOTE: When cutting hot peppers, disposable gloves are recommended. Avoid touching your face.

STRAWBERRIES 'N' CREAM
FRENCH TOAST STICKS

STRAWBERRIES 'N' CREAM FRENCH TOAST STICKS

YIELD: 4 SERVINGS

I like to watch my family's eyes open wide with delight when
they see this luscious French toast breakfast on the table.
The decadent dish is ready in a flash, but disappears even faster!

taryn kuebelbeck | plymouth, minnesota

- 1   container (16 ounces) frozen sweetened sliced strawberries, thawed
- 1/4 to 1/2 teaspoon ground cinnamon
- 1   teaspoon cornstarch
- 2   teaspoons water
- 1   package (12.7 ounces) frozen French toaster sticks
- 2   ounces cream cheese, softened
- 1-1/2 teaspoons brown sugar
- 1   square (1 ounce) white baking chocolate, melted and cooled

In a small saucepan, combine strawberries and cinnamon.
Combine cornstarch and water until smooth; stir into
berries. Bring to a boil; cook and stir for 2 minutes or until
thickened.

Prepare French toast sticks according to package directions.
Meanwhile, in a small bowl, beat the cream cheese and
brown sugar until light and fluffy. Stir in the melted chocolate.

Serve berry mixture over French toast; dollop with cream
cheese topping.

EDITOR'S NOTE: This recipe was tested with
Eggo French Toaster Sticks.

BANANA PANCAKES WITH BERRIES

YIELD: 4 SERVINGS

With strawberries, banana and a good buttermilk batter, this is my
family's all-time favorite pancake recipe for Saturday mornings.
I even serve these flavorful hotcakes for dinner occasionally
with some crispy bacon or a slice of country ham.

katie sloan | charlotte, north carolina

- 2   cups sliced fresh strawberries
- 1/2 cup sugar
- 3   teaspoons vanilla extract

PANCAKES:
- 1   cup all-purpose flour
- 1   tablespoon sugar
- 1   teaspoon baking powder
- 1/2 teaspoon baking soda
- 1/2 teaspoon salt
- 1   egg
- 1   cup buttermilk
- 2   tablespoons canola oil
- 1   teaspoon vanilla extract
- 2   medium ripe bananas, cut into 1/4-inch slices

Whipped cream, optional

In a bowl, combine the strawberries, sugar and vanilla. Cover
and refrigerate for 8 hours or overnight.

For pancakes, combine the flour, sugar, baking powder, baking
soda and salt in a bowl. Combine the egg, buttermilk, oil and
vanilla; stir into dry ingredients just until moistened.

Pour the batter by 1/4 cupfuls onto a lightly greased hot griddle;
place 5-6 banana slices on each pancake. Turn the pancakes
when bubbles form on top; cook until second side of pancake
is golden brown. Serve with strawberries and whipped cream
if desired.

BANANA PANCAKES WITH BERRIES

APPLE CARTWHEELS
YIELD: ABOUT 2 DOZEN

When you need to feed a group of children, try these stuffed apple rings. The yummy filling is a kid-friendly combination of creamy peanut butter, sweet honey, miniature chocolate chips and raisins.

miriam miller | thorp, wisconsin

1/4	cup peanut butter
1-1/2	teaspoons honey
1/2	cup miniature semisweet chocolate chips
2	tablespoons raisins
4	medium unpeeled Red Delicious apples, cored

In a bowl, combine peanut butter and honey; fold in the chocolate chips and raisins. Fill centers of apples with peanut butter mixture; refrigerate for at least 1 hour. Cut into 1/4-in. rings.

CHEESEBURGER PANCAKES
YIELD: 2 DOZEN

I combine the flavors of juicy cheeseburgers and freshly baked buns in this savory weekend specialty. Served with ketchup, a cheese sauce or cream of mushroom soup mixed with half-and-half, kids rave over having "cheeseburgers" for breakfast.

donna wenzel | monroe, michigan

1	pound ground beef
1/2	cup chopped onion
1/2	cup chopped celery
1/4	cup chopped green pepper
1	can (10-3/4 ounces) condensed tomato soup, undiluted
1	teaspoon Worcestershire sauce
1/2	teaspoon celery seed
1/4	teaspoon salt
1/8	teaspoon pepper
1	cup (4 ounces) shredded cheddar cheese

2	cups all-purpose flour
4	teaspoons baking powder
1	egg
1	cup milk

In a skillet, cook beef, onion, celery and green pepper until meat is no longer pink and vegetables are tender; drain. Stir in soup, Worcestershire sauce, celery seed, salt and pepper. Remove from the heat; cool slightly. Stir in cheese.

In a bowl, combine the flour and baking powder. Combine the egg and milk; stir into dry ingredients just until moistened. Add beef mixture; mix well. Pour batter by 1/4 cupfuls onto a lightly greased hot griddle. Cook for 4-6 minutes on each side or until golden brown.

HAM AND EGG PIZZA
YIELD: 6-8 SERVINGS

I make the most of a convenient prebaked pizza crust to create this delicious breakfast pie. Tasty toppings such as scrambled eggs, diced ham, crunchy water chestnuts, fresh tomatoes, ripe olives and shredded cheese provide plenty of pizzazz and a pretty presentation.

carol smith | wichita, kansas

1	cup cubed fully cooked ham
1	can (8 ounces) water chestnuts, drained and finely chopped
1	can (2-1/4 ounces) sliced ripe olives, drained
3	green onions, chopped
2	tablespoons butter
6	eggs
1/4	cup water

Salt and pepper to taste

1	prebaked Italian bread shell crust
1	medium tomato, seeded and diced
1/3	cup shredded part-skim mozzarella cheese
1/3	cup shredded cheddar cheese

In a large skillet, saute the ham, water chestnuts, olives and onions in butter until heated through. In a large bowl, whisk the eggs, water, salt and pepper; add to skillet. Cook over medium heat until eggs begin to set, stirring occasionally.

Place crust on a pizza pan or baking sheet; top with egg mixture. Sprinkle with tomato and cheeses. Bake at 425° for 7-10 minutes or until cheese is melted.

Breakfast TIP

I recently tried a recipe that called for chopped green onions. Instead of using a knife, I found that snipping the onions with a pair of kitchen scissors was faster and easier.

—Kristy B., Kelowna, British Columbia

SPECIAL OCCASION BREAKFASTS

CELEBRATE LIFE'S SPECIAL MOMENTS BY PLANNING THE ULTIMATE BRUNCH STARRING THESE SPECIALTIES.

HAM BUNDLES
PAGE 85

Looking for a quick and easy garnish that adds restaurant flair to your breakfast and brunch creations?

Instead of quartering fresh strawberries to accent homemade crepes, pancakes or waffles, slice the strawberries widthwise into disks to add a pretty decorative twist! The elegant presentation is sure to wow your guests.

BREAKFAST CREPES WITH BERRIES

After a long day of blackberry picking, I created a sauce to dress up some crepes I had on hand. The pretty dish makes an elegant addition to any brunch, and the sauce is delectable over warm waffles.

jennifer weisbrodt | oconomowoc, wisconsin

BREAKFAST CREPES WITH BERRIES
YIELD: 8 CREPES

1-1/2	cups fresh raspberries
1-1/2	cups fresh blackberries
1	cup (8 ounces) sour cream
1/2	cup confectioners' sugar
1	carton (6 ounces) orange creme yogurt
1	tablespoon lime juice
1-1/2	teaspoons grated lime peel
1/2	teaspoon vanilla extract
1/8	teaspoon salt
8	prepared crepes (9 inches)

In a large bowl, combine the raspberries and blackberries; set berries aside. In a small bowl, combine sour cream and confectioners' sugar until smooth. Stir in the yogurt, lime juice, lime peel, vanilla and salt.

Spread 2 tablespoons sour cream mixture over each crepe; top with about 1/3 cup berries. Roll up; drizzle with remaining sour cream mixture. Serve immediately.

HAM & ASPARAGUS
PUFF PANCAKE

YIELD: 6-8 SERVINGS

1/4	cup butter
1	cup all-purpose flour
4	eggs
1	cup milk
1/4	teaspoon salt
1/8	teaspoon white pepper

FILLING:

3/4	pound (1-1/2 cups) chopped fully cooked ham
1/2	pound fresh asparagus spears, trimmed and cut into 1-inch pieces
3	tablespoons butter
2	tablespoons all-purpose flour
3/4	cup milk
1/4	cup sour cream
1	teaspoon lemon juice
1/4	teaspoon hot pepper sauce
1/2	cup shredded cheddar cheese

Place the butter in a 10-in. ovenproof skillet; place in a 425° oven for 3-4 minutes or until melted. In a bowl, beat the flour, eggs, milk, salt and pepper until smooth. Pour the mixture into prepared skillet. Bake at 425° for 22-25 minutes or until puffed and golden brown.

Meanwhile, for filling, in a saucepan over medium-high heat, cook ham and asparagus in melted butter for 5 minutes, stirring occasionally. Stir in flour until blended. Gradually stir in milk. Bring to a boil; cook and stir for 3 minutes. Reduce heat; stir in sour cream, lemon juice and hot pepper sauce. Spoon filling into pancake. Sprinkle with cheese. Cut into wedges; serve immediately.

HAM & ASPARAGUS PUFF PANCAKE

Turn any morning into an extraordinary day by serving this fluffy and flavorful puff pancake filled with hearty ham and tender asparagus.

taste of home test kitchen

OMELET CASSEROLES

YIELD: 60 SERVINGS (4 CASSEROLES)

1	cup butter, melted
100	eggs
2-1/2	quarts milk
1-1/4	teaspoons white pepper
7-1/2	cups (30 ounces) shredded Swiss cheese
7-1/2	cups cubed fully cooked ham

Divide the butter among five 13-in. x 9-in. baking dishes; set aside. In a large bowl, beat 20 eggs, 2 cups milk and 1/4 teaspoon pepper until blended. Stir in 1-1/2 cups cheese and 1-1/2 cups ham; pour into one prepared dish. Repeat four times.

Bake, uncovered, at 350° for 40-45 minutes or until a knife inserted near the center comes out clean (cover with foil if the top browns too quickly). Let stand for 5 minutes before cutting.

OMELET CASSEROLES

Because this dish is so simple to make, it's ideal for church breakfasts or any time you need to feed a really big crowd. The Swiss cheese and diced ham add a nice flavor.

renee schwebach | dumont, minnesota

HARVEST VEGETABLE TART
YIELD: 6 SERVINGS

When folks lay eyes on this lightened-up veggie tart, oohs of approval start circling the table. I've been serving it for 30 years, and its robust taste and aroma always get a warm reception.

ruth lee | troy, ontario

- 1/2   cup all-purpose flour
- 1/4   cup whole wheat flour
- 1/4   cup cornmeal
- 2   tablespoons grated Parmesan cheese
- 1/2   teaspoon salt
- 1/8   teaspoon cayenne pepper
- 1/4   cup cold butter, cubed
- 3   to 4 tablespoons cold water

FILLING:
- 1/2   cup thinly sliced green onions
- 2   garlic cloves, minced
- 1   tablespoon olive oil
- 5   slices peeled eggplant (3-1/2 inches x 1/4 inch)
- 2   tablespoons grated Parmesan cheese, *divided*
- 1   small tomato, cut into 1/4-inch slices
- 3   green pepper rings
- 3   sweet red pepper rings
- 1/2   cup frozen corn
- 2   eggs, lightly beaten
- 2/3   cup fat-free evaporated milk
- 3/4   teaspoon salt
- 1/4   teaspoon pepper

In a bowl, combine the first six ingredients. Cut in butter until crumbly. Gradually add water, tossing with a fork until dough forms a ball. Cover and refrigerate for at least 30 minutes.

Roll out pastry to fit a 9-in. tart pan with removable bottom. Transfer pastry to pan; trim even with edge of pan. Line unpricked pastry shell with a double thickness of heavy-duty foil. Bake at 450° for 8 minutes. Remove foil; bake crust for 5 minutes longer.

For filling, in a large nonstick skillet coated with cooking spray, cook onions and garlic in oil for 2 minutes. Add eggplant; cook for 4-5 minutes or until softened. Cool for 5 minutes. Spoon into crust. Sprinkle with 1 tablespoon Parmesan cheese. Top with tomato slices and pepper rings. Sprinkle with corn.

In a small bowl, whisk the eggs, milk, salt and pepper; pour over vegetables. Sprinkle with remaining Parmesan cheese. Bake at 350° for 30-35 minutes or until a knife inserted near the center comes out clean.

CHOCOLATE DESSERT WAFFLES
YIELD: 4-6 WAFFLES

These yummy waffles add a sweet touch to any breakfast. I serve them on special occasions, and my guests always ask for the recipe.

phalice ayers | spokane, washington

- 1/4   cup butter, softened
- 1   cup sugar
- 2   eggs
- 2   squares (1 ounce *each*) unsweetened chocolate, melted and cooled
- 1   teaspoon vanilla extract
- 1-1/2   cups all-purpose flour
- 2   teaspoons baking powder
- 1/4   teaspoon salt
- 1/2   cup milk

Whipped cream, fresh fruit *or* ice cream

In a small bowl, cream butter and sugar until light and fluffy. Add eggs, one at a time, beating well after each addition. Stir in chocolate and vanilla. Combine the flour, baking powder and salt; add to the creamed mixture alternately with milk. Preheat waffle iron. Fill and bake according to manufacturer's directions. Serve with whipped cream, fruit or ice cream.

BROCCOLI QUICHE CREPE CUPS

BROCCOLI QUICHE CREPE CUPS
YIELD: 4 SERVINGS

When I was very young and just learning to cook, this was one of the first recipes I made. I still make these and my children do, too!

kristin arnett | elkhorn, wisconsin

- 1-1/2 cups milk
- 3 eggs
- 1 cup all-purpose flour
- 1/4 teaspoon salt
- FILLING:
- 1 package (10 ounces) frozen broccoli with cheese sauce
- 3 bacon strips, diced
- 1/2 cup chopped onion
- 2 eggs
- 1/4 cup milk

In a blender, combine the milk, eggs, flour and salt; cover and process until smooth. Cover and refrigerate for 1 hour.

Heat a lightly greased 8-in. nonstick skillet over medium heat; pour 2 tablespoons batter into the center of skillet. Lift and tilt pan to coat bottom evenly. Cook until top appears dry; turn and cook 15-20 seconds longer. Remove to a wire rack. Repeat with remaining batter, greasing skillet as needed. When cool, stack crepes with waxed paper or paper towels in between.

Line each of four 6-oz. custard cups with a crepe; set aside. Freeze remaining crepes in a freezer bag, leaving waxed paper between each crepe, for up to 3 months.

For filling, cook broccoli according to package directions. Cut up any larger pieces of broccoli. In a microwave-safe bowl, microwave bacon on high for 2 minutes; drain. Add the onion; microwave on high for 3 minutes or until tender. Beat eggs and milk; stir in broccoli mixture and bacon mixture. Spoon into prepared crepe cups.

Bake, uncovered, at 350° for 30-35 minutes or until a knife inserted near the center comes out clean. Remove from custard cups and serve immediately.

CHRISTMAS MORNING PIE
YIELD: 12-16 SERVINGS

Nothing spreads holiday cheer like this cheesy breakfast pie. Its warm, comforting flavor is extra delicious on Christmas morning.

sally harlan | charleston, south carolina

- 1 pound bulk pork sausage, cooked and drained
- 1 cup (4 ounces) shredded Swiss cheese
- 1 cup (4 ounces) shredded cheddar cheese
- 2 unbaked pastry shells (9 inches)
- 6 eggs, lightly beaten
- 1 cup milk
- 1/2 cup chopped onion
- 1/3 cup chopped sweet red pepper
- 1/3 cup chopped green pepper

In a large bowl, combine sausage and cheeses. Place half of mixture in each pastry shell.

In a large bowl, combine eggs, milk, onion and peppers. Pour half over sausage in each shell. Bake at 350° for 55-60 minutes or until a knife inserted near the center comes out clean. Let stand 5 minutes before cutting.

CREAM-TOPPED GRAPES

CREAM-TOPPED GRAPES
YIELD: 8 SERVINGS

I dress up bunches of red and green grapes with a decadent dressing that comes together in a jiffy. You can also dollop the heavenly four-ingredient sauce over your favorite combination of fruit.

vioda geyer | uhrichsville, ohio

- 4 ounces cream cheese, softened
- 1/4 cup sugar
- 1/2 teaspoon vanilla extract
- 1/2 cup sour cream
- 3 cups seedless green grapes
- 3 cups seedless red grapes

In a small bowl, beat the cream cheese, sugar and vanilla. Add the sour cream; mix well. Divide grapes among individual serving bowls; dollop with topping.

HAM BUNDLES

HAM BUNDLES
YIELD: 2 DOZEN

Whenever I serve ham, I can't wait for the leftovers so I can make these tasty nibbles. My husband often warms them up for breakfast.

chris sendelbach | henry, illinois

1	package (1/4 ounce) active dry yeast
1/4	cup warm water (110° to 115°)
3/4	cup warm milk (110° to 115°)
1/2	cup shortening
3	eggs, lightly beaten
1/2	cup sugar
1-1/2	teaspoons salt
4-1/2	to 4-3/4 cups all-purpose flour

FILLING:

1	large onion, finely chopped
5	tablespoons butter, *divided*
4	cups cubed fully cooked ham, coarsely ground
4	bacon strips, cooked and crumbled, optional
1/4	to 1/3 cup sliced pimiento-stuffed olives, optional
1/2	to 3/4 cup shredded cheddar cheese, optional

In a large bowl, dissolve yeast in warm water. Add the milk, shortening, eggs, sugar, salt and 2 cups flour; beat until smooth. Add enough remaining flour to form a soft dough.

Turn onto a lightly floured surface; knead until smooth and elastic, about 8 minutes. Place in a greased bowl, turning once to grease top. Cover and let rise in a warm place until doubled, about 1 hour.

Meanwhile, for filling, in a large skillet, saute onion in 2 tablespoons butter until tender. Add ham and mix well; set aside.

Punch dough down. Turn onto a lightly floured surface; divide into thirds. Roll each portion into a 16-in. x 8-in. rectangle. Cut each rectangle into eight squares. Place a tablespoonful of ham mixture in the center of each square. Add bacon, olives and/or cheese if desired. Fold up corners to center of dough; seal edges.

Place 2 in. apart on greased baking sheets. Cover and let rise in a warm place until doubled, about 45 minutes.

Melt remaining butter; brush over dough. Bake at 350° for 16-20 minutes or until golden brown and filling is heated through. Refrigerate leftovers.

PLUM SAUSAGE BITES
YIELD: 18-22 SERVINGS

Packed with perky flavor and a thick sauce that clings to the sausage, these links are a must for my special occasion brunches and potlucks. They're ready in no time, which adds to their appeal.

heidi fisher | victoria, british columbia

2	to 2-1/2 pounds uncooked pork sausage links, cut into 1-inch pieces
1	cup plum, apple *or* grape jelly
2	tablespoons soy sauce
1	tablespoon Dijon mustard

In a large skillet, cook sausage over medium heat until no longer pink; drain and set sausage aside. In the same skillet, stir in the jelly, soy sauce and mustard. Simmer, uncovered, for 5 minutes, stirring occasionally. Return sausage to the pan and heat through. Refrigerate any leftovers.

DUTCH HONEY SYRUP
YIELD: 2 CUPS

I grew up on a farm where a big breakfast was an everyday occurrence. Still, it was a wonderful treat when Mom served this scrumptious syrup with a stack of golden pancakes.

kathy scott | hemingford, nebraska

1	cup sugar
1	cup corn syrup
1	cup heavy whipping cream
1	teaspoon vanilla extract

In a saucepan, combine sugar, corn syrup and cream. Bring to a boil over medium heat; boil for 5 minutes or until slightly thickened, stirring occasionally. Stir in vanilla. Serve warm over pancakes, waffles or French toast.

Breakfast TIP

Perk up ordinary maple syrup with this simple trick. Stir 1 to 2 tablespoons of orange marmalade into a cup of warm maple syrup. It makes it so special.

—Helen G., Dover, New Hampshire

CHICKEN CORDON BLEU CREPES
YIELD: 7 SERVINGS

I created these savory crepes as a way to use up leftover chicken and ham. It's an easy, but elegant dish for company.

susan kemmerer | telford, pennsylvania

- 1   cup all-purpose flour
- 2   eggs
- 1-1/4   cups milk

FILLING:
- 2   cups coarsely chopped cooked chicken
- 2/3   cup chopped fully cooked ham
- 1   cup (4 ounces) shredded Swiss cheese

SAUCE:
- 2   tablespoons butter
- 2   tablespoons all-purpose flour
- 1   teaspoon chicken bouillon granules
- 1-1/2   cups milk
- 1/4   cup shredded Swiss cheese
- 2   tablespoons chopped fully cooked ham

Minced fresh parsley

In a bowl, whisk the flour, eggs and milk until smooth. Cover and refrigerate for 1 hour.

Heat a lightly greased 7-in. skillet. Pour about 2 tablespoons batter into the center of skillet; lift and tilt pan to evenly coat bottom. Cook until top appears dry; turn and cook 15-20 seconds longer. Remove to a plate. Repeat with remaining batter, adding oil to the skillet as needed. Place waxed paper between crepes.

To fill crepes, sprinkle chicken, ham and Swiss cheese over each. Roll up tightly. Place seam side down in a greased 13-in. x 9-in. baking dish.

For sauce, in a small saucepan, melt butter. Stir in the flour and bouillon until blended. Gradually whisk in milk. Bring to a boil; cook and stir for 1-2 minutes or until thickened and bubbly. Remove from the heat. Stir in Swiss cheese and ham until cheese is melted. Pour 2/3 cup sauce over crepes.

Bake, uncovered, at 350° for 15-20 minutes or until bubbly and heated through. Sprinkle with fresh parsley. Serve with remaining sauce.

CHICKEN CORDON BLEU CREPES

CRAB-SPINACH EGG CASSEROLE

CRAB-SPINACH EGG CASSEROLE
YIELD: 12-16 SERVINGS

I've developed a strong interest in cooking over the years. I came up with this delightfully different casserole as a special breakfast for our daughter when she was home for a visit.

steve heaton | deltona, florida

- 8   eggs
- 2   cups half-and-half cream
- 2   cans (6 ounces *each*) crabmeat, drained
- 1   package (10 ounces) frozen chopped spinach, thawed and squeezed dry
- 1   cup dry bread crumbs
- 1   cup (4 ounces) shredded Swiss cheese
- 1/2   teaspoon salt
- 1/4   teaspoon pepper
- 1/4   teaspoon ground nutmeg
- 2   celery ribs, chopped
- 1/2   cup chopped onion
- 1/2   cup chopped sweet red pepper
- 3   medium fresh mushrooms, chopped
- 2   tablespoons butter

In a large bowl, beat eggs and cream. Stir in the crab, spinach, bread crumbs, cheese, salt, pepper and nutmeg; set aside. In a skillet, saute the celery, onion, red pepper and mushrooms in butter until tender. Add to the spinach mixture.

Transfer to a greased shallow 2-1/2-qt. baking dish. Bake, uncovered, at 375° for 30-35 minutes or until golden brown around the edges and center is set. Let stand for 10 minutes before serving.

Breakfast TIP

When using fresh mushrooms in a recipe, such as Crab-Spinach Egg Casserole, gently remove dirt by wiping them with a damp paper towel. Do not peel mushrooms. Then trim stems and use as directed in the recipe.

HOLIDAY STRATA
YIELD: 6 SERVINGS

The layers of favorite breakfast ingredients will have folks digging into this all-in-one dish. The hearty combination of eggs, ham and cheese creates just the right focal point for an Easter brunch, although we've been known to enjoy the delicious dish by itself, too.

dorothy smith | el dorado, arkansas

8	slices bread, crusts removed and cubed
1/4	cup minced fresh parsley
1	green onion, sliced
1	cup cubed fully cooked ham
1	cup (4 ounces) shredded Swiss cheese
3	eggs
2	cups milk
2	teaspoons Dijon mustard
1/8	teaspoon salt
1/8	teaspoon pepper
1/8	teaspoon hot pepper sauce

Place half of the bread cubes in a greased 11-in. x 7-in. baking dish. Sprinkle with half of the parsley, onion, ham and cheese. Repeat layers.

In a large bowl, whisk the eggs, milk, mustard, salt, pepper and hot pepper sauce. Pour over cheese. Bake, uncovered, at 350° for 35-40 minutes or until a knife inserted near the center comes out clean.

HOLIDAY STRATA

BREAKFAST KUGEL
YIELD: 12 SERVINGS

Noodle dishes are high on my family's list of favorites. In fact, they could eat lasagna any time of day. This is like a breakfast lasagna that we serve at every family brunch.

carol miller | northumberland, new york

3	cups (24 ounces) 4% cottage cheese
1	teaspoon vanilla extract
1/4	teaspoon salt
5	medium tart apples, peeled and thinly sliced
1	teaspoon ground cinnamon
2	cups applesauce
2	cups raisins
1	package (16 ounces) lasagna noodles, cooked and drained
1	cup (4 ounces) shredded cheddar cheese

In a blender, combine the cottage cheese, vanilla and salt; cover and process until smooth. Toss apples with cinnamon. Combine applesauce and raisins; spread 3/4 cup into a greased 13-in. x 9-in. baking dish.

Layer with a fourth of the lasagna noodles, and a third of the applesauce mixture, cottage cheese mixture and apples. Repeat layers twice. Top with remaining noodles; sprinkle with cheddar cheese. Cover and bake at 350° for 60-70 minutes or until apples are tender. Let stand for 15 minutes before cutting.

FRUIT-FILLED PUFF PANCAKE
YIELD: 4 SERVINGS

The mixture of cinnamon, blueberries and bananas is heavenly. If you're expecting just a few guests for breakfast, try this!

leanne senger | oregon city, oregon

1	tablespoon butter
1/3	cup all-purpose flour
3	tablespoons sugar, *divided*
1/4	teaspoon salt
3	eggs, lightly beaten
1/2	cup milk
1-1/2	cups fresh *or* frozen blueberries
1	medium ripe banana, sliced
1/4	teaspoon ground cinnamon

Place butter in a 9-in. pie plate. Bake at 400° for 4-5 minutes or until melted. Meanwhile, in a large bowl, combine the flour, 1 tablespoon sugar and salt. Add eggs and milk; whisk until smooth.

Pour into hot pie plate. Bake at 400° for 10-12 minutes or until edges are puffed and golden brown. Meanwhile, combine blueberries and banana. In a small bowl, combine cinnamon and remaining sugar. Spoon fruit mixture onto pancake; sprinkle with cinnamon-sugar. Cut into wedges.

FRUIT-FILLED PUFF PANCAKE

HOLIDAY BREAKFAST STRUDELS

HOLIDAY BREAKFAST STRUDELS
YIELD: 10 SERVINGS

Instead of a typical egg bake, we came up with this elegant entree where an individual phyllo dough strudel features a flavorful Swiss and Parmesan cheese sauce and a hearty pork sausage filling.

taste of home test kitchen

1/4	cup butter
1/4	cup all-purpose flour
2	cups milk
2/3	cup shredded Swiss cheese
1/4	cup grated Parmesan cheese
1	teaspoon salt
1/4	teaspoon ground nutmeg

Dash pepper

1/2	pound bulk pork sausage
10	eggs, beaten
1	teaspoon dried thyme
2	teaspoons dried parsley flakes

PASTRY:

20	sheets phyllo dough (14 inches x 9 inches)
1	cup butter, melted
1/2	cup dry bread crumbs

TOPPING:

1/4	cup grated Parmesan cheese

Minced fresh parsley

In a large saucepan, melt butter. Stir in flour until smooth; gradually add milk. Bring to a boil; cook and stir for 2 minutes or until thickened. Stir in the cheeses, salt, nutmeg and pepper. Cook and stir until cheese is melted; set aside.

Crumble sausage into a skillet; cook over medium heat until no longer pink. Drain. Add eggs and thyme; cook and stir gently until eggs are completely set. Stir into cheese sauce; add parsley. Cool completely.

For pastry, carefully unroll phyllo dough. Place one sheet of phyllo on a sheet of waxed paper (keep remaining dough covered with plastic wrap to avoid drying out). Brush with butter; sprinkle lightly with bread crumbs. Top with a second sheet of phyllo; brush with butter. Spread 1/2 cup egg mixture along the short side of dough to within 1 in. of edges. Beginning from the filled end, fold short side over filling. Fold

in sides and roll up. Place seam side down on an ungreased baking sheet. Repeat nine times.

For the topping, combine Parmesan cheese and parsley. Brush each roll with butter; sprinkle with topping. Bake at 350° for 15-20 minutes or until crisp and lightly browned. Serve strudels immediately.

EGG 'N' PEPPERONI BUNDLES
YIELD: 4 SERVINGS

My family calls these "one more gift to open" because it's the last present they unwrap on Christmas morning. Everyone's mouth waters when they bite into these delicious, flaky bundles loaded with our favorite breakfast ingredients.

helen meadows | trout creek, montana

7	sheets phyllo dough (14 inches x 9 inches)
1/2	cup butter, melted
8	teaspoons dry bread crumbs
2	ounces cream cheese, cut into 8 cubes
4	eggs
24	slices pepperoni, quartered *or* 1-1/2 ounces Canadian bacon, diced
1/3	cup provolone cheese
2	teaspoons minced chives

Place one sheet of phyllo dough on a work surface; brush with butter. Top with another sheet of phyllo; brush with butter. Repeat five times. Cut phyllo in half widthwise, then cut in half lengthwise. Carefully place one stack in each of four greased jumbo muffin cups. Brush edges of dough with butter. Sprinkle 2 teaspoons of bread crumbs onto the bottom of each cup. Top the bread crumbs with two cubes of cream cheese each.

Break each egg separately into a custard cup; gently pour egg over cream cheese. Sprinkle with pepperoni, provolone cheese and chives. Pinch corners of phyllo together to seal. Bake at 400° for 13-17 minutes or until golden brown. Serve warm.

NEW YEAR'S RAISIN FRITTERS
YIELD: 6 DOZEN

Those who enjoy raisins will love these special, sweet fritters, which have been a traditional New Year's celebration treat in our family for at least five generations.

jaycille zart | kamloops, british columbia

1	tablespoon active dry yeast
1/2	cup warm water (110° to 115°)
2	teaspoons plus 1/4 cup sugar, *divided*
2	cups warm milk (110° to 115°)
1/4	cup butter, melted
1-1/2	teaspoons salt
2	eggs

4 to 4-1/2 cups all-purpose flour
1 package (15 ounces) raisins
Oil for frying
Additional sugar

In a large bowl, dissolve yeast in warm water. Add 2 teaspoons sugar; let stand for 5 minutes. Add the milk, butter, salt, eggs, remaining sugar and 2 cups flour. Beat until smooth. Stir in enough remaining flour to form a thick batter. Stir in raisins. Cover and let rise in a warm place until doubled, about 1 hour.

Stir down batter; cover and let rise again until doubled. In an electric skillet or deep-fat fryer, heat oil to 375°. Drop batter by tablespoonfuls, a few at a time, into hot oil. Fry until golden brown on both sides. Drain on paper towels. Roll in additional sugar while warm.

CREPE QUICHE CUPS

SAUSAGE EGG SQUARES
YIELD: 12 SERVINGS

Chock-full of sausage and cheese, this fluffy, baked egg dish is an absolute winner any time of day. Our four children and six grandkids request it often whenever they visit.

myrna duke | chelan, washington

1 pound turkey Italian sausage links, casings removed
1 medium green pepper, chopped
1 small onion, chopped
2 cups (16 ounces) 1% cottage cheese
2 cups (8 ounces) shredded reduced-fat cheddar cheese
1-1/2 cups egg substitute
1 cup fat-free milk
1 cup reduced-fat biscuit/baking mix
1 can (4 ounces) chopped green chilies

In a large nonstick skillet, cook sausage, green pepper and onion over medium heat until meat is no longer pink; drain. stir in the remaining ingredients. Pour into a 13-in. x 9-in. baking dish coated with cooking spray. Bake at 350° for 35-40 minutes or until a knife inserted near the center comes out clean. Let stand for 10 minutes before cutting.

SAUSAGE EGG SQUARES

CREPE QUICHE CUPS
YIELD: 16 CREPE CUPS

I enjoy trying new recipes, especially when I know I'll be entertaining family and friends. These wonderfully different crepe cups hold an enticing sausage, egg and cheese filling.

sheryl riley | unionville, missouri

2 eggs
1 cup plus 2 tablespoons milk
2 tablespoons butter, melted
1 cup all-purpose flour
1/8 teaspoon salt
FILLING :
1/2 pound bulk pork sausage
1/4 cup chopped onion
3 eggs
1/2 cup milk
1/2 cup mayonnaise
2 cups (8 ounces) shredded cheddar cheese

For crepe batter, in a small bowl, beat the eggs, milk and butter. Combine flour and salt; add to egg mixture and mix well. Cover and refrigerate for 1 hour.

For filling, in a small skillet, cook sausage and onion over medium heat until meat is no longer pink; drain. In a large bowl, whisk the eggs, milk and mayonnaise. Stir in sausage mixture and cheese; set aside.

Heat a lightly greased 8-in. nonstick skillet. Stir crepe batter; pour 2 tablespoons into center of skillet. Lift and tilt pan to coat bottom evenly. Cook until top appears dry; turn and cook 15-20 seconds longer.

Remove to a wire rack. Repeat with remaining batter, greasing skillet as needed. When cool, stack crepes with waxed paper in between each crepe.

Line greased muffin cups with crepes; fill two-thirds full with sausage mixture. Bake at 350° for 15 minutes. Cover loosely with foil; bake 10-15 minutes longer or until a knife inserted near the center comes out clean.

RASPBERRY FRENCH TOAST CUPS
YIELD: 2 SERVINGS

These individual treats are a delightful twist on French toast that make any morning special. I made this recipe for my mom last Mother's Day, and we both enjoyed it.

sandi tuttle | hayward, wisconsin

  2   slices Italian bread, cut into 1/2-inch cubes
1/2   cup fresh *or* frozen raspberries
  2   ounces cream cheese, cut into 1/2-inch cubes
  2   eggs
1/2   cup milk
  1   tablespoon maple syrup

RASPBERRY SYRUP:

  2   teaspoons cornstarch
1/3   cup water
  2   cups fresh *or* frozen raspberries, *divided*
  1   tablespoon lemon juice
  1   tablespoon maple syrup
1/2   teaspoon grated lemon peel
Ground cinnamon, optional

Divide half of the bread cubes between two greased 8-oz. custard cups. Sprinkle with raspberries and cream cheese. Top with remaining bread. In a small bowl, whisk the eggs, milk and syrup; pour over bread. Cover and refrigerate for at least 1 hour.

Remove from the refrigerator 30 minutes before baking. Bake, uncovered, at 350° for 25-30 minutes or until the bread crumbs are golden brown.

Meanwhile, for the syrup, in a small saucepan, combine the cornstarch and water until smooth. Add 1-1/2 cups fresh raspberries, lemon juice, syrup and lemon peel. Bring to a boil; reduce heat. Cook and stir for 2 minutes or until the syrup thickened. Strain and discard seeds; cool slightly.

Gently stir the remaining berries into syrup. Sprinkle French toast cups with cinnamon if desired; serve with syrup.

RASPBERRY FRENCH TOAST CUPS

BAKED FRUIT MEDLEY
YIELD: 3-4 SERVINGS

Years ago, I would make breakfast for my staff at work. This comforting casserole was always on the menu.

patricia swanson | cabot, arkansas

  1   can (29 ounces) pear halves
  1   can (11 ounces) mandarin oranges, drained
  1   teaspoon grated lime peel
1/3   cup packed brown sugar
1/4   cup flaked coconut

Drain pears, reserving 1/2 cup juice; set juice aside. Place pears, oranges and lime peel in an ungreased 11-in. x 7-in. baking dish. Combine brown sugar and pear juice; stir until sugar is dissolved. Pour over fruit. Sprinkle with coconut. Bake, uncovered, at 350° for 25-30 minutes or until heated through. Serve warm or chilled.

SAN JOSE TORTILLA PIE
YIELD: 10-12 SERVINGS

Because my husband is in the Navy, we've lived in many parts of the country and have had the great opportunity to try different foods in each region. This is a family favorite, especially when it is served with fried potatoes and fresh fruit.

anne boesiger | billings, montana

  6   corn tortillas (6 inches)
Oil for deep-fat frying
Salt
  1   pound ground beef
  1   large onion, chopped
  1   medium green pepper, chopped
  1   garlic clove, minced
  1   tablespoon chili powder
  1   tablespoon dried oregano
  1   teaspoon ground cumin
  2   cups (8 ounces) shredded cheddar cheese
  1   to 2 cans (4 ounces *each*) chopped green chilies
  6   eggs
1-1/2   cups milk
1/2   teaspoon salt
Sliced ripe olives, optional

Cut each tortilla into eight wedges. Saute a few at a time in hot oil until crisp. Drain on paper towels; sprinkle with salt.

In a large skillet, cook ground beef, onion, green pepper and garlic until beef is no longer pink and vegetables are tender; drain. Stir in chili powder, oregano, and cumin.

In a greased 13-in. x 9-in. baking dish, layer half of the tortilla wedges, half the meat mixture and half the cheddar cheese. Tuck the remaining tortilla wedges, point side up, around the edge of dish.

In a small bowl, beat eggs, milk and salt. Pour evenly over top. Bake, uncovered, at 375° for 25-30 minutes. Garnish with olives if desired.

BROCCOLI-HAM CHEESE PIE

BROCCOLI-HAM
CHEESE PIE
YIELD: 6 SERVINGS

Sheets of easy-to-use phyllo dough create a crisp, buttery crust for this daybreak entree. The egg and vegetable pie always gets a two-thumbs-up approval from my sons and husband.

nancy granaman | burlington, iowa

12	sheets phyllo dough (14 inches x 9 inches)

Refrigerated butter-flavored spray

1	package (16 ounces) frozen broccoli cuts, thawed and patted dry
1	cup cubed fully cooked lean ham
1	cup (4 ounces) shredded reduced-fat cheddar cheese
1	small onion, chopped
2	tablespoons minced fresh parsley
2	garlic cloves, minced
1/2	teaspoon dried thyme
1/2	teaspoon salt
1/2	teaspoon pepper
1	cup egg substitute
1	cup fat-free evaporated milk
2	tablespoons grated Parmesan cheese

Spritz one sheet of phyllo dough with butter-flavored spray. Place in a 9-in. pie plate coated with cooking spray; allow one end of dough to overhang edge of plate by 3-4 in. (Until ready to use, keep phyllo dough covered with plastic wrap and a damp towel to prevent drying out.) Repeat with remaining phyllo, overlapping the sheets (staggering the points around the plate) and spritzing with butter-flavored spray between each layer.

In a large bowl, combine the broccoli, ham, cheese, onion, parsley, garlic, thyme, salt and pepper; spoon into crust. Combine egg substitute and milk; pour over broccoli mixture. Fold edges of dough over filling toward center of pie plate. Spritz edges with butter-flavored spray.

Cover edge of crust with foil. Bake at 375° for 40 minutes. Remove foil. Sprinkle with Parmesan cheese. Bake 30-35 minutes longer or until a knife inserted near the center comes out clean. Let stand for 10 minutes before cutting.

ITALIAN SAUSAGE
CASSEROLE
YIELD: 12 SERVINGS

At the start of each week, my gang is already looking forward to our traditional weekend breakfasts, when I serve warm and wonderful dishes such as this. The make-ahead convenience lets me relax with the family as the savory aroma fills the house.

nancy robinson | kansas city, kansas

1	pound bulk pork sausage
1	pound bulk Italian sausage
1	medium green pepper, chopped
1	cup sliced fresh mushrooms
1/2	cup chopped onion
2-1/2	cups onion and garlic croutons
8	eggs
1-1/2	cups milk
1	cup (4 ounces) shredded part-skim mozzarella cheese
1	cup (4 ounces) shredded cheddar cheese
3	to 4 Roma tomatoes, thinly sliced
1/2	cup Parmesan cheese, shredded

In a large skillet, cook sausage, green pepper, mushrooms and onion until meat is browned and vegetables are tender; drain. Place croutons in a greased 13-in. x 9-in. baking dish; top with sausage mixture. Beat eggs and milk; pour over sausage. Cover and chill for 8 hours or overnight. Remove from refrigerator 30 minutes before baking. Bake, uncovered, at 300° for 1 hour.

Sprinkle with the mozzarella and cheddar cheeses. Place tomato slices over top; sprinkle with Parmesan cheese. Bake 20 minutes longer or until a knife inserted near the center comes out clean. Let stand 5 minutes before cutting.

ITALIAN SAUSAGE CASSEROLE

Breakfast TIP

PHYLLO (pronounced FEE-lo) is a tissue-thin pastry that's made by gently stretching the dough into thin, fragile sheets. It can be layered, shaped and baked in a variety of ways. Handling it quickly is the key!

PHILLY BEEF 'N' PEPPER STRATA

PHILLY BEEF 'N' PEPPER STRATA
YIELD: 12 SERVINGS

Here's a mouthwatering entree for brunch, lunch or dinner that's quick to fix. It combines several convenient ingredients for a large casserole that's pleasing to all who try it.

betty claycomb | alverton, pennsylvania

7	cups cubed Italian bread
3-3/4	cups julienned sweet red, yellow *and/or* green peppers
1/4	cup chopped onion
3/4	pound cooked roast beef, cut into thin strips
2	cups (8 ounces) shredded Monterey Jack cheese
8	eggs
2-1/4	cups milk
2	tablespoons Dijon mustard
1/2	teaspoon salt
1/2	teaspoon pepper

Place a third of the bread cubes in a greased 13-in. x 9-in. baking dish. Layer with a third of the peppers, onion, roast beef and cheese. Repeat layers twice. In a large bowl, whisk the eggs, milk, mustard, salt and pepper; pour over top. Cover and refrigerate for 8 hours or overnight.

Remove from the refrigerator 30 minutes before baking. Bake, covered, at 325° for 1 hour. Uncover; bake 15-20 minutes longer or until a knife inserted near the center comes out clean. Let stand for 10 minutes before serving.

SLUSH FRUIT CUPS
YIELD: 20 SERVINGS

I try to have some of these fruit cups in my freezer all the time so I can serve them to my family for breakfast or to unexpected company at any time of the day. The refreshing blend of flavors and pretty color add festive flair to any table.

lynn schumacher | grant, nebraska

1	can (20 ounces) crushed pineapple
1	package (10 ounces) frozen strawberries in juice, thawed
1	can (6 ounces) frozen orange juice concentrate, thawed
3/4	cup thawed lemonade concentrate
3	firm bananas, cut into 1/4-inch slices
1-1/2	cups lemon-lime soda
1	cup water
1	cup sugar
20	paper cups (5 ounces)

In a large bowl, mix the pineapple, strawberries, orange juice concentrate, lemonade concentrate, bananas, soda, water and sugar.

Pour about 1/2 cup into each paper cup. Cover with foil and freeze until firm. Remove from freezer 15 minutes before serving. Serve in a dessert cup.

EDITOR'S NOTE: For 10 servings, pour fruit mixture by 1/3 cupfuls into paper-lined muffin cups.

CHICKEN BROCCOLI CREPES
YIELD: 8 CREPES

When I organized food and nutrition training for our county 4-H'ers, we had cooking demonstrations representing different countries. We chose crepes for France, and everyone devoured them when stuffed with this chicken and broccoli filling.

deanna naivar | temple, texas

1	cup plus 2 tablespoons milk
2	eggs
2	tablespoons butter, melted
1	cup all-purpose flour
1/4	teaspoon salt

FILLING:

1/4	cup butter
1/4	cup all-purpose flour
2	cups chicken broth
2	teaspoons Worcestershire sauce
3	cups (12 ounces) shredded cheddar cheese, *divided*
2	cups (16 ounces) sour cream
2	packages (8 ounces *each*) frozen broccoli spears, cooked and drained
2-1/2	cups cubed cooked chicken

In a small bowl, beat the milk, eggs and butter. Combine flour and salt; add to egg mixture and beat until smooth. Cover and refrigerate for 1 hour.

Heat a lightly greased 8-in. nonstick skillet. Stir batter; pour 1/4 cup into the center of skillet. Lift and tilt pan to evenly coat bottom. Cook until top appears dry; turn and cook 15-20 seconds longer. Remove to a wire rack. Repeat with remaining batter, greasing skillet as needed. When cool, stack crepes with waxed paper or paper towels in between each crepe.

For filling, in a large saucepan, melt butter. Stir in the flour until smooth. Gradually stir in broth and Worcestershire sauce. Bring to a boil; cook and stir for 2 minutes or until thickened. Reduce heat; stir in 2 cups of shredded cheddar cheese. Cook and stir for 10 minutes or until the cheese is melted. Remove mixture from the heat; stir in sour cream until smooth.

Place four broccoli spears and 1/3 cup of chicken down the center of each crepe; top with 1/3 cup cheese sauce. Roll up and place seam side down in a greased 13-in. x 9-in. baking dish. Pour remaining cheese sauce over crepes; sprinkle with remaining cheese. Bake, uncovered, at 350° for 20 minutes or until heated through.

CHICKEN BROCCOLI CREPES

EGGSQUISITE BREAKFAST CASSEROLE
YIELD: 12-16 SERVINGS

I developed this recipe over 20 years ago. The rich, warm sauce tastes especially good on cold winter mornings. I hope your family enjoys this satisfying bake as much as mine does!

bee fischer | jefferson, wisconsin

1	pound sliced bacon, diced
2	packages (4-1/2 ounces *each*) sliced dried beef, cut into thin strips
1	can (4-1/2 ounces) sliced mushrooms
1/2	cup all-purpose flour
1/8	teaspoon pepper
4	cups milk
16	eggs
1	cup evaporated milk
1/4	teaspoon salt
1/4	cup butter, cubed

Chopped fresh parsley, optional

In a large skillet, cook bacon until crisp. Remove bacon to paper towels to drain; discard all but 1/4 cup drippings. In the same skillet, add the beef, mushrooms, flour and pepper to the drippings; cook until thoroughly combined. Gradually add milk; cook and stir until thickened. Stir in bacon; set aside.

In a large bowl, whisk eggs, evaporated milk and salt. In another large skillet, heat butter until hot. Add egg mixture; cook and stir over medium heat until eggs are completely set.

Place half of the eggs in a greased 13-in. x 9-in. baking dish; pour half the sauce over the eggs. Repeat layers. Cover and bake at 300° for 45-50 minutes or until heated through. Let stand 5 minutes before serving.

POTLUCK EGGS BENEDICT
YIELD: 10-12 SERVINGS

This hearty breakfast dish is super served over warm, fluffy biscuits. Folks can't wait to dig into the creamy, savory combination of eggs, ham, cheddar cheese and asparagus.

pauline van breemen | franklin, indiana

1	pound fresh asparagus, trimmed
3/4	cup butter, cubed
3/4	cup all-purpose flour
4	cups milk
1	can (14-1/2 ounces) chicken broth
1	pound cubed fully cooked ham
1	cup (4 ounces) shredded cheddar cheese
8	hard-cooked eggs, quartered
1/2	teaspoon salt
1/8	teaspoon cayenne pepper
10	to 12 biscuits, warmed

Cut asparagus into 1/2-in. pieces, using only tender parts of spears. Cook in a small amount of boiling water until tender, about 5 minutes; drain. Set aside to cool.

Melt butter in a saucepan; stir in flour until smooth. Add milk and broth; bring to a boil. Cook and stir for 2 minutes. Add ham and cheese; stir until cheese is melted. Add eggs, salt, cayenne and asparagus; heat through. Serve over biscuits.

POTLUCK EGGS BENEDICT

ALMOND FRENCH TOAST HEARTS
YIELD: 3 SERVINGS

On Valentine's Day, I like to surprise my family at breakfast by having heart-shaped French toast on the table. Confectioners' sugar, strawberries and almond butter tastefully top off each bite.

donna cline | *pensacola, florida*

- 6 slices bread
- 2 eggs
- 1/4 cup milk
- 1-1/2 teaspoons almond extract, *divided*
- 2 tablespoons plus 1 cup butter, *divided*
- 3 tablespoons confectioners' sugar
- Additional confectioners' sugar
- Sliced fresh strawberries

Cut out bread slices with a 3-3/4-in. heart-shaped cookie cutter; discard trimmings.

In a shallow bowl, combine the eggs, milk and 1/2 teaspoon almond extract. Dip bread on both sides in egg mixture. In a large skillet, melt 2 tablespoons butter. Fry bread hearts until golden brown on both sides.

For almond butter, in a small bowl, combine confectioners' sugar and remaining butter and extract; mix well. Sprinkle French toast with additional confectioners' sugar. Serve with almond butter and sliced fresh strawberries.

BLACK HILLS GOLDEN EGG BAKE

BLACK HILLS GOLDEN EGG BAKE
YIELD: 10-12 SERVINGS

I developed this recipe when I was cooking for large groups of people on a regular basis. It's easy to make and gives you plenty of time to do other things while it's baking.

sandra giardino | *rapid city, south dakota*

- 1/2 cup sliced fresh mushrooms
- 1/2 cup chopped green pepper
- 1/4 cup butter, cubed
- 10 eggs
- 1/2 cup all-purpose flour
- 1 teaspoon baking powder
- 1/4 teaspoon salt, optional
- 2 cups (16 ounces) 4% cottage cheese
- 2 cups (8 ounces) shredded cheddar cheese
- 2 cups (8 ounces) shredded Monterey Jack cheese
- 1/2 pound bulk pork sausage, cooked and drained
- 6 bacon strips, cooked and crumbled
- 1 can (2-1/4 ounces) sliced ripe olives, drained

In a small skillet, saute mushrooms and green pepper in butter until tender. In a large bowl, combine the eggs, flour, baking powder and salt if desired. Add mushroom mixture. Stir in remaining ingredients.

Pour into a greased 13-in. x 9-in. baking dish. Bake, uncovered, at 400° for 15 minutes. Reduce heat to 350°; bake 25-35 minutes longer or until a knife inserted near the center comes out clean.

CURRIED EGGS IN SHRIMP SAUCE
YIELD: 12 SERVINGS

I like to dress up leftover hard-cooked eggs from Easter with a special shrimp sauce. It's a real time-saver as you can assemble this casserole the day before and bake it the next morning.

m. beatrice mann | *vernon, vermont*

- 3 tablespoons butter, *divided*
- 2 tablespoons all-purpose flour
- 1 can (10-3/4 ounces) condensed cream of shrimp soup, undiluted
- 1 cup milk
- 1/2 cup shredded cheddar cheese
- 1/2 pound frozen cooked small shrimp, thawed and chopped
- 12 hard-cooked eggs
- 1/2 cup mayonnaise
- 1/4 teaspoon curry powder
- 1/4 teaspoon ground mustard
- 1/4 teaspoon paprika
- 1/8 teaspoon salt
- 1 cup soft bread crumbs

In a large saucepan, melt 2 tablespoons butter; whisk in flour until smooth. Gradually add soup and milk. Bring to a boil; cook and stir over medium heat for 2 minutes or until thickened. Remove from the heat; stir in cheddar cheese until melted. Stir in the shrimp.

Pour 2 cups of sauce into a greased 13-in. x 9-in. baking dish; set remaining sauce aside. Cut eggs in half lengthwise. Arrange egg whites over sauce; in a bowl, mash yolks. Stir in the mayonnaise, curry powder, mustard, paprika and salt. Spoon into egg whites. Top with reserved sauce.

Melt the remaining butter; toss with bread crumbs. Sprinkle over the top. Bake, uncovered, at 350° for 15-20 minutes or until heated through.

HEART-SHAPED COFFEE CAKE

HEART-SHAPED COFFEE CAKE
YIELD: 2 COFFEE CAKES

You'll love to make this pretty coffee cake for your sweetheart on special occasions and anniversaries. It's almost too pretty to eat.

norma hammond | leland, iowa

1	package (1/4 ounce) active dry yeast
1/4	cup warm water (110° to 115°)
1	cup warm milk (110° to 115°)
3/4	cup butter, melted, *divided*
2	eggs, beaten
1/4	cup sugar
1	teaspoon salt
3-1/2	to 4 cups all-purpose flour

FILLING:

1/2	cup sugar
1/2	cup finely chopped walnuts
2	teaspoons ground cinnamon

ICING:

2	tablespoons butter, softened
2	cups confectioners' sugar
1	teaspoon vanilla extract
5	to 6 tablespoons milk

In a bowl, dissolve yeast and water. Add milk, 1/2 cup butter, eggs, sugar, salt and 2 cups of flour. Add enough remaining flour to form a soft dough. Turn onto a floured surface; knead until smooth and elastic, about 6-8 minutes. Place in a greased bowl; turn once to grease top. Cover and let rise in a warm place until doubled, about 1 hour.

Punch dough down; let rest for 10 minutes. Divide in half. On a floured surface, roll each portion into a 15-in. x 10-in. rectangle. Brush with remaining butter. Combine the filling ingredients; sprinkle over each rectangle to within 1/2 in. of the edges.

Roll up jelly-roll style, starting with a long side; pinch seams to seal. Place, seam side up, on two greased baking sheets. Fold each roll in half lengthwise with seams touching, with one side 1-1/2 in. longer than the other.

With scissors, make a lengthwise cut down the middle to within 1 in. of open ends. Open and lay flat; arrange into a heart shape. Cover and let rise until doubled, about 30 minutes.

Bake at 350° for 15-20 minutes or until golden brown. Cool on wire racks. For icing, in a small bowl, cream butter, sugar and vanilla; add milk. Drizzle over hearts.

PEAR-PECAN SAUSAGE QUICHE
YIELD: 8 SERVINGS

This unique quiche would be a delightful addition to brunch, especially during the holiday season. It's savory from the sausage yet sweet from the sliced pear.

patricia harmon | baden, pennsylvania

1/2	pound bulk hot Italian sausage
1/3	cup chopped sweet onion
1	medium pear, sliced
1	pastry shell (9 inches)
1/3	cup chopped pecans
4	eggs
1-1/2	cups half-and-half cream
1/2	teaspoon salt
1/2	teaspoon dried thyme
1/8	teaspoon ground nutmeg
1	cup (4 ounces) shredded cheddar cheese
8	pecan halves

In a large skillet, cook sausage and onion over medium heat for 4-5 minutes or until meat is no longer pink; drain. Arrange pear slices in crust; top with sausage. Sprinkle with pecans. In a large bowl, whisk the eggs, cream, salt, thyme and nutmeg. Stir in cheese. Pour over sausage.

Bake at 350° for 35-40 minutes or until a knife inserted near the center comes out clean and crust is golden brown. Garnish the quiche with pecan halves. Let quiche stand for 5 minutes before slicing.

Breakfast TIP

To avoid water on the bottom of the pie when making a quiche, use an oven thermometer to check your oven temperature. Then, to avoid overbaking, do the "knife test" when the quiche appears to have set around the edges but still seems a little soft in the very center. The quiche is done if the knife inserted near the center comes out clean.

BREADS & SWEET TREATS

WAKE UP TO THE AROMA OF FRESHLY BAKED LOAVES, MUFFINS, SCONES AND OTHER MADE-FROM-SCRATCH DELIGHTS.

ORANGE-RHUBARB
BREAKFAST BREAD
PAGE 99

Breakfast TIP

If you won't be eating your baked creations right away, cool coffee cake and sweet rolls completely. Then place them in an airtight container or plastic bag. They'll keep at room temperature for 2 to 3 days. (However, breads containing perishable items should be refrigerated.) For longer storage, unfrosted breads will freeze for up to 3 months.

PEACH COBBLER COFFEE CAKE

"Absolutely delicious" is how people describe this comforting coffee cake that features peaches and a delectable frosting. Serve it warm for an extra-special treat.

virginia krites | cridersville, ohio

PEACH COBBLER COFFEE CAKE
YIELD: 12 SERVINGS

1	cup butter, softened
1	cup sugar
2	eggs
3	teaspoons vanilla extract
3	cups all-purpose flour
1	teaspoon baking powder
1	teaspoon baking soda
1/2	teaspoon salt
1-1/4	cups sour cream
1	can (21 ounces) peach pie filling
1	can (15-1/4 ounces) sliced peaches, drained

TOPPING:

1	cup packed brown sugar
1	cup all-purpose flour
1/2	cup quick-cooking oats
1/4	teaspoon ground cinnamon
1/2	cup cold butter, cubed

GLAZE:

1	cup confectioners' sugar
1	to 2 tablespoons milk

In a large bowl, cream butter and sugar until light and fluffy. Add eggs, one at a time, beating well after each addition. Beat in the vanilla. Combine flour, baking powder, baking soda and salt; add to creamed mixture alternately with sour cream. Beat just until combined.

Pour half of the batter into a greased 13-in. x 9-in. baking dish. Combine the pie filling and peaches; spread over batter. Drop remaining batter by tablespoonfuls over filling.

For topping, combine the brown sugar, flour, oats and cinnamon in a bowl. Cut in butter until mixture is crumbly. Sprinkle over batter.

Bake at 350° for 70-75 minutes or until a toothpick inserted near the center comes out clean. Cool on a wire rack. Combine glaze ingredients; drizzle over coffee cake.

ROYAL RHUBARB COFFEE CAKE

ROYAL RHUBARB COFFEE CAKE
YIELD: 15 SERVINGS

1/3	cup butter, softened
1	cup sugar
1	egg
1	teaspoon vanilla extract
2	cups all-purpose flour
3	teaspoons baking powder
1/2	teaspoon salt
1	cup milk
3-1/2	cups chopped fresh *or* frozen rhubarb, thawed and drained

TOPPING:

3/4	cup packed brown sugar
1/4	cup butter, melted
1	teaspoon ground cinnamon

In a large bowl, cream butter and sugar until light and fluffy. Beat in egg and vanilla. Combine the flour, baking powder and salt; gradually add to creamed mixture alternately with milk, beating well after each addition.

Pour into a greased 13-in. x 9-in. baking dish. Spoon the rhubarb to within 1/2 in. of edges. Combine topping ingredients; sprinkle over top.

Bake at 350° for 45-55 minutes or until a toothpick inserted near the center comes out clean. Cool on a wire rack.

EDITOR'S NOTE: If using frozen rhubarb, measure rhubarb while still frozen, then thaw completely. Drain rhubarb in a colander, but do not press liquid out.

You'll often find this delectable coffee cake on my table in spring when there is an abundance of rhubarb. For another twist, you can use raspberries and blueberries in place of the rhubarb with equally delicious results.

lorraine robinson | *stony plain, alberta*

SPICED PEAR BREAD
YIELD: 4 MINI LOAVES (6 SLICES EACH)

3-1/4	cups all-purpose flour
1	cup sugar
3	teaspoons ground cinnamon
1	teaspoon baking soda
1	teaspoon baking powder
1	teaspoon ground cloves
1/2	teaspoon salt
3	eggs
3	cans (15-1/4 ounces *each*) sliced pears, drained and mashed
1/4	cup unsweetened applesauce
1/4	cup canola oil

In a large bowl, combine the first seven ingredients. In a small bowl, whisk the eggs, pears, applesauce and canola oil. Stir the egg mixture into dry ingredients just until moistened.

Pour into four 5-3/4-in. x 3-in. loaf pans coated with cooking spray. Bake at 350° for 50-60 minutes or until a toothpick inserted near the center comes out clean. Cool loaves for 10 minutes before removing from pans to wire racks to cool completely.

SPICED PEAR BREAD

I can my own pears, so I always have plenty on hand when I want to make this wonderful bread. It's hard not to have another slice…or two…of this moist loaf.

rachel barefoot | *linden, michigan*

ORANGE-RHUBARB BREAKFAST BREAD

YIELD: 1 LOAF (16 SLICES)

I love starting my day with a slice of this fabulous quick bread alongside eggs, sausage and orange juice. Each piece is full of tangy flavor and crunchy slivered almonds.

sonya goergen | moorhead, minnesota

1/3	cup butter, softened
1	cup sugar
2	eggs
1	teaspoon vanilla extract
2	cups all-purpose flour
1-1/2	teaspoons baking powder
1/2	teaspoon baking soda
1/2	teaspoon salt
1/4	teaspoon ground ginger
1/4	teaspoon ground nutmeg
1/2	cup orange juice
1	cup chopped fresh *or* frozen rhubarb
1/2	cup slivered almonds
2	teaspoons grated orange peel

In a large bowl, cream butter and sugar until light and fluffy. Add eggs, one at a time, beating well after each addition. Beat in vanilla.

Combine the flour, baking powder, baking soda, salt, ginger and nutmeg; add to creamed mixture alternately with orange juice. Fold in the rhubarb, almonds and orange peel.

Transfer to a greased 9-in. x 5-in. loaf pan. Bake at 350° for 55-65 minutes or until a toothpick inserted near the center comes out clean. Cool for 10 minutes before removing from pan to a wire rack.

EDITOR'S NOTE: If using frozen rhubarb, measure rhubarb while still frozen, then thaw completely. Drain in a colander, but do not press liquid out.

COCONUT-GLAZED ORANGE SCONES

YIELD: 1-1/2 DOZEN

Guaranteed to brighten up gloomy winter afternoons, these yummy scones created by our home economists offer a refreshing tropical zing with the flavors of orange and coconut. A simply elegant glaze completes the light, melt-in-your-mouth treats with sweet results.

taste of home test kitchen

3-3/4	cups self-rising flour
1/4	cup sugar
2	teaspoons baking powder
1/2	cup cold butter
2	eggs
1	cup plus 1 to 2 tablespoons milk, *divided*
1	teaspoon grated orange peel
1/2	cup confectioners' sugar
1/4	teaspoon coconut extract

In a large bowl, combine the flour, sugar and baking powder. Cut in butter until mixture resembles coarse crumbs. In a small bowl, whisk eggs, 1 cup milk and orange peel; stir into crumb mixture just until moistened. Turn onto a floured surface; knead 10 times.

Roll into a 14-in. x 8-in. rectangle. Using a floured pizza cutter, cut widthwise into 2-in. strips, then cut diagonally into 2-in. strips, forming diamond shapes. Place 2 in. apart on baking sheets coated with cooking spray. Bake at 400° for 8-10 minutes or until lightly browned. Remove to wire racks.

For glaze, in a small bowl, combine the confectioners' sugar, coconut extract and enough remaining milk to achieve desired consistency; drizzle over scones. Serve warm.

EDITOR'S NOTE: As a substitute for self-rising flour, place 5-1/2 teaspoons baking powder and 1-3/4 teaspoons salt in a measuring cup. Add all-purpose flour to measure 1 cup. Add another 2-3/4 cups all-purpose flour to the bowl.

LONG JOHNS
YIELD: 2-1/2 DOZEN

The tattered and torn card in my files is a good indication of how popular these doughnuts have been in our family over the years. The tender, glazed bites disappear in a hurry, so I typically make a double batch.

twilla eisele | wellsville, kansas

1	package (1/4 ounce) active dry yeast
1/4	cup warm water (110° to 115°)
1	cup warm milk (110° to 115°)
1/4	cup butter, softened
1/4	cup sugar
1/2	teaspoon salt
1	egg
3-1/4	to 3-3/4 cups all-purpose flour

Oil for frying

GLAZE:

1-1/4	cups confectioners' sugar
1	tablespoon brown sugar
1	tablespoon water
1/2	teaspoon vanilla extract
1/8	teaspoon salt

In a large bowl, dissolve yeast in warm water. Add the milk, butter, sugar, salt and egg and 2 cups flour. Beat until smooth. Stir in enough flour to form a soft dough.

Do not knead. Place dough in a greased bowl, turning once to grease top. Cover and let rise in a warm place until doubled, about 1 hour.

Punch dough down. Turn onto a lightly floured surface; roll into a 12-in. x 8-in. rectangle. Cut into 3-in. x 1-in. rectangles. Place on greased baking sheets. Cover and let rise in a warm place until doubled, about 30 minutes.

In an electric skillet or deep-fat fryer, heat oil to 400°. Fry doughnuts, a few at a time, until golden brown on both sides. Drain on paper towels. Combine glaze ingredients. Dip tops in glaze while warm.

LONG JOHNS

PUFFS WITH HONEY BUTTER

PUFFS WITH HONEY BUTTER
YIELD: 5 DOZEN

A priest gave me the recipe for these delicious doughnut-like puffs. With yummy honey butter spread on top, the puffs are just as good at breakfast functions as they are as a snack or sweet appetizer at evening get-togethers.

ruth plaushin | swiftwater, pennsylvania

1/4	cup plus 3 tablespoons butter, softened, *divided*
1/4	cup honey
3	eggs
1	carton (8 ounces) plain yogurt
2	cups all-purpose flour
2	teaspoons baking powder
1	teaspoon baking soda
1/2	teaspoon ground nutmeg
1/4	teaspoon salt

Oil for frying

In a large bowl, combine 1/4 cup butter and honey until smooth; set side.

In a large bowl, beat eggs until lemon-colored. Beat in yogurt and remaining butter until smooth. Combine the flour, baking powder, baking soda, nutmeg and salt; stir dry ingredients into yogurt mixture.

In a deep-fat fryer or electric skillet, heat oil to 360°. Drop batter by teaspoonfuls into oil. Fry until golden brown, about 1 minute on each side. Drain on paper towels. Serve warm with the honey butter.

KEY LIME BREAD
YIELD: 2 LOAVES

I first tasted this unusual, but wonderful, breakfast bread at a friend's house, and she graciously shared the recipe with me. The tropical-inspired loaf is easy to make and absolutely scrumptious!

joan hallford | north richland hills, texas

2/3	cup butter, softened
2	cups sugar
4	eggs
2	tablespoons grated lime peel

2 tablespoons key lime juice
1 teaspoon vanilla extract
3 cups all-purpose flour
3 teaspoons baking powder
1 teaspoon salt
1 cup milk
1 cup chopped walnuts

GLAZE:
2/3 cup confectioners' sugar
1 to 2 tablespoons key lime juice

In a large bowl, cream butter and sugar. Add eggs; mix well. Add lime peel, juice and vanilla; mix until combined. Combine the flour, baking powder and salt; add to creamed mixture alternately with milk. Fold in walnuts.

Transfer to two greased 9-in. x 5-in. loaf pans. Bake at 350° for 50-55 minutes or until a toothpick inserted near the center comes out clean. Cool for 10 minutes before removing from pans to wire racks.

Combine the glaze ingredients; drizzle over the warm bread. Let bread cool completely.

HAM AND CHEESE MUFFINS
YIELD: ABOUT 1 DOZEN

These savory, biscuit-like muffins are fantastic in the morning with coffee or in the afternoon with a hearty bowl of soup.

doris heath | *bryson city, north carolina*

2 cups self-rising flour
1/2 teaspoon baking soda
1 cup milk
1/2 cup mayonnaise
1/2 cup finely chopped fully cooked ham
1/2 cup shredded cheddar cheese

In a large bowl, combine flour and baking soda. Combine remaining ingredients; stir into the dry ingredients just until moistened. Fill greased or paper-lined muffin cups two-thirds full. Bake at 425° for 16-18 minutes or until muffins test done.

> **EDITOR'S NOTE:** As a substitute for each cup of self-rising flour, place 1-1/2 teaspoons baking powder and 1/2 teaspoon salt in a measuring cup. Add all-purpose flour to measure 1 cup.

Breakfast TIP

Using a spoon to fill muffin cups with batter can get messy. To quickly put the batter into muffin cups with little mess, our home economists suggest using an ice cream scoop with a quick release.

CINNAMON CHIP RAISIN SCONES
YIELD: 15 SCONES

This creative morning favorite features raisins and homemade cinnamon "chips" to produce rich, mouth-watering scones. I think they're best served warm with lemon curd or butter and jelly.

mary ann morgan | *cedartown, georgia*

CINNAMON CHIPS:
3 tablespoons sugar
1 tablespoon ground cinnamon
2 teaspoons shortening
2 teaspoons corn syrup

SCONES:
1-2/3 cups bread *or* all-purpose flour
2 tablespoons sugar
2 teaspoons baking powder
1/2 teaspoon salt
1/3 cup cold butter
1/2 cup evaporated milk
1/2 cup raisins
Additional evaporated milk

In a large bowl, combine the sugar, cinnamon, shortening and corn syrup with a fork until crumbly and evenly blended. Spread onto a foil-lined baking sheet. Bake at 250° for 30-40 minutes or until melted and bubbly. Cool completely; break into small pieces.

In a large bowl, combine the flour, sugar, baking powder and salt. Cut in butter until the mixture resembles coarse crumbs. Stir in evaporated milk just until moistened. Gently stir in raisins and cinnamon chips. Turn dough onto a lightly floured surface. Roll to 1/2-in. thickness; cut with a floured 2-in. biscuit cutter.

Line a baking sheet with foil and grease the foil. Place the scones 1 in. apart on foil. Brush the tops lightly with additional evaporated milk. Bake at 400° for 14-16 minutes or until golden brown. Serve the scones warm.

CINNAMON CHIP RAISIN SCONES

CHERRY CREAM CHEESE COFFEE CAKE

CHERRY CREAM CHEESE COFFEE CAKE
YIELD: 8-10 SERVINGS

You'll like the flaky texture of this luscious coffee cake. The sour cream pairs well with the cherries, and the crunchy almonds add a nice accent. With a sweet streusel topping, it's hard to eat only one slice.

linda guiles | belvidere, new jersey

2-1/4	cups all-purpose flour
3/4	cup sugar
3/4	cup cold butter, cubed
1/2	teaspoon baking powder
1/2	teaspoon baking soda
1/2	teaspoon salt
1	egg, lightly beaten
3/4	cup sour cream
1	teaspoon almond extract

FILLING:

1	package (8 ounces) cream cheese, softened
1/4	cup sugar
1	egg, lightly beaten
1	can (21 ounces) cherry pie filling
1/2	cup slivered almonds

In a large bowl, combine flour and sugar. Cut in butter until crumbly. Reserve 3/4 cup crumb mixture. Add the baking powder, baking soda and salt to remaining crumb mixture. Stir in the egg, sour cream and almond extract until blended. Press onto the bottom and 1 in. up the sides of an ungreased 9-in. springform pan with removable bottom.

For filling, in a large bowl, beat the cream cheese and sugar for 1 minute. Add egg; beat just until combined. Spread over crust. Carefully top with pie filling. Sprinkle with almonds and reserved crumb mixture.

Bake at 350° for 50-60 minutes or until center is set. Cool on a wire rack. Carefully run a knife around edge of pan to loosen; remove sides of pan. Store in the refrigerator.

MOIST BRAN MUFFINS
YIELD: 4 MUFFINS

If you think bran muffins are dry and bland, you haven't tried these delectable bites. Topped with honey or cream cheese, these moist muffins are a wonderful and healthful way to start your day.

mildred ross | badin, north carolina

1/2	cup All-Bran
1/2	cup milk
2	tablespoons canola oil
1/2	cup all-purpose flour
2	tablespoons sugar
1	teaspoon baking powder
1/4	teaspoon salt

In a large bowl, combine the bran and milk; let stand for 5 minutes. Stir in the oil. Combine the remaining ingredients; stir into bran mixture just until moistened.

Fill greased or paper-lined muffin cups half full. Bake at 400° for 18-22 minutes or until a toothpick comes out clean. Cool for 5 minutes before removing from pan to a wire rack.

CINNAMON FRUIT BISCUITS
YIELD: 10 SERVINGS

Because these sweet gems are so easy, I'm almost embarrassed when people ask me for the recipe—it's just refrigerated buttermilk biscuits, sugar, cinnamon and fruit preserves.

ione burham | washington, iowa

1/2	cup sugar
1/2	teaspoon ground cinnamon
1	tube (12 ounces) refrigerated buttermilk biscuits, separated into 10 biscuits
1/4	cup butter, melted
10	teaspoons strawberry preserves

In a small bowl, combine sugar and cinnamon. Dip top and sides of biscuits in butter, then in cinnamon-sugar.

Place on ungreased baking sheets. With the end of a wooden spoon handle, make a deep indentation in the center of each biscuit; fill with 1 teaspoon preserves. Bake at 375° for 15-18 minutes or until golden brown. Cool for 15 minutes before serving (preserves will be hot).

CINNAMON FRUIT BISCUITS

POPPY SEED LEMON SCONES

POPPY SEED LEMON SCONES
YIELD: 8 SCONES

You'll love the appealing look and delicate texture of these slightly sweet scones. They're absolutely heavenly served warm with homemade lemon curd for breakfast or with a salad for lunch.

linda murray | allenstown, new hampshire

LEMON CURD:
- 2 eggs
- 1 cup sugar
- 6 tablespoons butter, melted
- 1/4 cup lemon juice
- 2 tablespoons grated lemon peel

SCONES:
- 2 cups all-purpose flour
- 1/4 cup sugar
- 1 tablespoon poppy seeds
- 2 teaspoons baking powder
- 1/2 teaspoon baking soda
- 1/4 teaspoon salt
- 1/3 cup cold butter
- 3/4 cup milk
- 2 tablespoons lemon juice

Additional sugar

In a heavy saucepan or top of a double boiler, beat eggs and sugar. Stir in butter, lemon juice and peel. Cook and stir over low heat or simmering water for 15 minutes or until mixture reaches 160° and is thickened. Cover and refrigerate until chilled (may be stored in the refrigerator for up to 1 week).

For scones, combine the flour, sugar, poppy seeds, baking powder, baking soda and salt in a bowl. Cut in butter until mixture resembles fine crumbs. Combine milk and lemon juice; stir milk mixture into crumb mixture just until blended (dough will be soft).

Turn dough onto a floured surface; knead gently six times. Shape into a ball. Pat dough into an 8-in. circle; cut into eight wedges. Separate wedges and place 1 in. apart on a greased baking sheet. Sprinkle with additional sugar. Bake at 425° for 12-15 minutes or until lightly browned. Remove from pan to wire rack. Serve the scones warm with the lemon curd.

BERRY-FILLED DOUGHNUTS
YIELD: 10 SERVINGS

Just four ingredients are all you'll need for this sure-to-be-popular morning treat. Friends and family will never guess that buttermilk biscuits are the base for these golden, jelly-filled doughnuts.

ginny watson | broken arrow, oklahoma

- 4 cups canola oil
- 1 tube (7-1/2 ounces) refrigerated buttermilk biscuits, separated into 10 biscuits
- 3/4 cup seedless strawberry jam
- 1 cup confectioners' sugar

In an electric skillet or deep-fat fryer, heat oil to 375°. Fry biscuits, a few at a time, for 1-2 minutes on each side or until golden brown. Drain on paper towels.

Cut a small hole in the corner of a pastry or plastic bag; insert a very small tip. Fill bag with jam. Push the tip through the side of each doughnut to fill with jam. Dust with confectioners' sugar while warm. Serve immediately.

BLUEBERRY OAT MUFFINS
YIELD: 1 DOZEN

Looking for a tasty alternative to cereal or toast? Try these moist, fruity and tender muffins. Each bite is so full of blueberry and oat flavor that no one believes they are low in fat.

mildred mummau | mt. joy, pennsylvania

- 1-1/4 cups all-purpose flour
- 1 cup quick-cooking oats
- 1/2 cup sugar
- 1 teaspoon baking powder
- 1/2 teaspoon baking soda
- 1/4 teaspoon salt
- 2 egg whites
- 1/2 cup water
- 1/3 cup canola oil
- 1 cup fresh *or* frozen blueberries

TOPPING:
- 2 tablespoons sugar
- 1/4 teaspoon ground cinnamon

In a bowl, combine the first six ingredients. In another bowl, beat egg whites, water and oil. Stir into dry ingredients just until moistened. Fold in blueberries.

Fill paper-lined muffin cups or muffin cups coated with cooking spray three-fourths full. Combine the sugar and cinnamon; sprinkle over muffins.

Bake at 400° for 18-22 minutes or until a toothpick inserted near the center comes out clean. Cool muffins for 5 minutes before removing them from the pan to a wire rack.

EDITOR'S NOTE: If using frozen blueberries, do not thaw blueberries before adding to batter.

CAPPUCCINO MUFFINS
YIELD: ABOUT 14 MUFFINS (1 CUP SPREAD)

Not only are these chocolate and coffee muffins great for breakfast, they make a tasty dessert or midnight snack. Serve them with a cup of freshly brewed coffee or a tall glass of cold milk.

janice bassing | racine, wisconsin

ESPRESSO SPREAD:
- 4 ounces cream cheese, cubed
- 1 tablespoon sugar
- 1/2 teaspoon instant coffee granules
- 1/2 teaspoon vanilla extract
- 1/4 cup miniature semisweet chocolate chips

MUFFINS:
- 2 cups all-purpose flour
- 3/4 cup sugar
- 2-1/2 teaspoons baking powder
- 1 teaspoon ground cinnamon
- 1/2 teaspoon salt
- 1 cup milk
- 2 tablespoons instant coffee granules
- 1/2 cup butter, melted
- 1 egg
- 1 teaspoon vanilla extract
- 3/4 cup miniature semisweet chocolate chips

In a food processor or blender, combine the espresso spread ingredients; cover and process until well blended. Transfer to a small bowl; cover and refrigerate until serving.

In a large bowl, combine the flour, sugar, baking powder, cinnamon and salt. In another bowl, stir milk and coffee granules until coffee is dissolved. Add butter, egg and vanilla; mix well. Stir into dry ingredients just until moistened. Fold in chocolate chips.

Fill greased or paper-lined muffin cups two-thirds full. Bake at 375° for 17-20 minutes or until a toothpick inserted near the center comes out clean. Cool for 5 minutes before removing from pans to wire racks. Serve muffins with espresso spread.

CAPPUCCINO MUFFINS

ORANGE-RAISIN STICKY MUFFINS

ORANGE-RAISIN STICKY MUFFINS
YIELD: 1 DOZEN

A batch of these muffins has the appeal of old-fashioned sticky buns without the fuss of yeast dough. The delightful blend of flavors comes from walnuts, raisins, cinnamon and a sunny orange zest. They're a sure eye-opener and a welcomed treat anytime.

sandi ritchey | silverton, oregon

- 1/4 cup chopped raisins
- 1 tablespoon sugar
- 1/2 teaspoon ground cinnamon

TOPPING:
- 1/2 cup chopped nuts
- 1/3 cup packed brown sugar
- 2 tablespoons butter, melted
- 2 tablespoons honey
- 1/4 teaspoon ground cinnamon

MUFFINS:
- 2 cups all-purpose flour
- 3 teaspoons baking powder
- 1/2 teaspoon salt
- 1 egg
- 2/3 cup milk
- 1/4 cup honey
- 1/3 cup butter, melted
- 2 tablespoons grated orange peel

Combine raisins, sugar and cinnamon; set aside. Combine the topping ingredients and spoon 1 teaspoonful into 12 greased muffin cups. Set aside.

In a bowl, combine the flour, baking powder and salt. Beat egg, milk, honey, butter and orange peel; stir into dry ingredients just until moistened. Spoon 1 tablespoon of batter into the prepared muffin cups; sprinkle with raisin mixture. Top with remaining batter.

Bake at 375° for 16-20 minutes or until muffins test done. Cool for 5 minutes; invert pan onto a lightly buttered foil-lined shallow baking pan. Serve warm.

ZUCCHINI BANANA BREAD
YIELD: 3 MINI LOAVES (6 SLICES EACH)

1-1/2	cups all-purpose flour
1	cup sugar
1	teaspoon ground cinnamon
1/2	teaspoon baking powder
1/2	teaspoon baking soda
1/2	teaspoon salt
1	egg
1	cup mashed ripe bananas
1/2	cup canola oil
1/2	teaspoon banana extract
1/2	teaspoon vanilla extract
1	cup shredded zucchini
1/2	cup chopped walnuts

In a large bowl, combine the first six ingredients. In a small bowl, beat the egg, bananas, oil and extracts. Stir into the dry ingredients just until moistened. Fold in zucchini and walnuts.

Transfer to three 5-3/4-in. x 3-in. loaf pans coated with cooking spray. Bake at 325° for 40-45 minutes or until a toothpick inserted near the center comes out clean. Cool the loaves for 10 minutes before removing from pans to wire racks.

ZUCCHINI BANANA BREAD

I got this recipe from a friend at work and now it's one I treasure. I've found it to be a delicious way to use up extra zucchini from the garden. It makes three small loaves that are perfect for freezing or gift giving.

donna hall | wolfforth, texas

BUTTERMILK DOUGHNUTS

It doesn't take long for a platter of these doughnuts to vanish. Our grandkids go for them in a big way! The cinnamon-sugar topping is out of this world!

betty rauschendorfer | sidney, montana

BUTTERMILK DOUGHNUTS
YIELD: 4 DOZEN

4	eggs
2	cups sugar
1/3	cup butter, melted
1	teaspoon vanilla extract
5-1/2	to 6 cups all-purpose flour
2	teaspoons baking powder
2	teaspoons baking soda
1	teaspoon salt
1	teaspoon ground nutmeg
2	cups buttermilk

Oil for frying
Additional sugar, cinnamon-sugar *or* confectioners' sugar, optional

In a large bowl, beat eggs and sugar until light and lemon-colored. Add butter and vanilla; mix well. Combine the flour, baking powder, baking soda, salt and nutmeg; add to egg mixture alternately with buttermilk. Cover and refrigerate for 2-3 hours.

On a lightly floured surface, roll dough to 1/2-in. thickness. Cut with a floured 3-in. doughnut cutter.

In an electric skillet or deep-fat fryer, heat oil to 375°. Fry doughnuts, a few at a time, for 1 minute on each side or until golden. Drain on paper towels. Roll in additional sugar if desired.

CRANBERRY SURPRISE MUFFINS

CRANBERRY SURPRISE MUFFINS
YIELD: 1 DOZEN

This recipe has been in my family since 1943, so these muffins have appeared during the holidays for many years. The "surprise" is a dollop of cranberry sauce in the center. We think the best way to eat the tender morsels is warm, fresh from the oven.

helen howley | *mount laurel, new jersey*

2	cups all-purpose flour
2	tablespoons sugar
3	teaspoons baking powder
1/2	teaspoon salt
2	eggs
1	cup milk
1/4	cup butter, melted
1	cup jellied cranberry sauce

In a large bowl, combine the flour, sugar, baking powder and salt. In another bowl, whisk the eggs, milk and butter. Stir into dry ingredients just until moistened.

Fill 12 greased muffin cups one-fourth full. Drop a rounded tablespoonful of cranberry sauce into each cup. Top with remaining batter.

Bake at 400° for 12-15 minutes or until muffin tops spring back when lightly touched. Cool for 5 minutes before removing from pan to a wire rack. Serve warm.

EDITOR'S NOTE: These muffins are best served the day they're made.

POPPY SEED DOUGHNUTS
YIELD: 6 SERVINGS

This scrumptious doughnut recipe from our home economists provides a few extra servings but freezes well. Though you may find it difficult not to eat them all at once!

taste of home test kitchen

1	cup all-purpose flour
1/2	cup sugar
1	tablespoon poppy seeds
3/4	teaspoon baking powder
3/4	teaspoon baking soda
1/4	teaspoon salt
1	egg
1/3	cup buttermilk
1/3	cup reduced-fat plain yogurt
1	tablespoon canola oil
2	teaspoons lemon juice
1	teaspoon grated lemon peel
1/2	teaspoon vanilla extract
2	teaspoons confectioners' sugar, *divided*

In a small bowl, combine the first six ingredients. Combine the egg, buttermilk, yogurt, oil, lemon juice, peel and vanilla; stir into dry ingredients just until moistened.

Coat six 4-in. tube pans with cooking spray and dust with 1 teaspoon confectioners' sugar. Divide batter among pans.

Bake at 400° for 10-12 minutes or until a toothpick inserted near the center comes out clean. Cool for 5 minutes before removing from pans to wire racks. Dust with remaining confectioners' sugar.

PUMPKIN GINGER SCONES
YIELD: 8 SCONES

I made these lovely scones one day when looking for a way to use up leftover pumpkin, and I was not disappointed. To simplify things, I often use my food processor to stir up the dough just until it comes together. It works great!

brenda jackson | *garden city, kansas*

2	cups all-purpose flour
7	tablespoons plus 1 teaspoon sugar, *divided*
2	teaspoons baking powder
1	teaspoon ground cinnamon
1/2	teaspoon salt
1/2	teaspoon ground ginger
1/4	teaspoon baking soda
5	tablespoons cold butter, *divided*
1	egg, lightly beaten
1/4	cup canned pumpkin
1/4	cup sour cream

In a large bowl, combine the flour, 7 tablespoons sugar, baking powder, cinnamon, salt, ginger and baking soda. Cut in 4 tablespoons butter until mixture resembles coarse crumbs. Combine the egg, pumpkin and sour cream; stir into dry ingredients just until moistened.

Turn the dough onto a floured surface; knead 10 times. Pat dough into an 8-in. circle. Cut into eight wedges. Separate wedges and place on a greased baking sheet. Melt the remaining butter; brush over the wedges. Sprinkle with the remaining sugar. Bake at 425° for 15-20 minutes or until golden brown. Serve warm.

COFFEE LOVER'S COFFEE CAKE
YIELD: 9 SERVINGS

I had this deliciously different coffee cake at a friend's brunch, and she graciously shared the recipe. Now people always request it from me because they know it will be a hit with guests.

gale lalmond | deering, new hampshire

1/3	cup sugar
4-1/2	teaspoons instant coffee granules
1-1/2	teaspoons ground cinnamon

BATTER:

3	tablespoons butter, softened
1/2	cup sugar
1	egg
1	teaspoon vanilla extract
1-1/2	cups all-purpose flour
1	teaspoon baking powder
1/2	teaspoon baking soda
1/8	teaspoon salt
1	cup (8 ounces) plain yogurt
2	tablespoons chopped walnuts *or* pecans

In a small bowl, combine the sugar, coffee granules and cinnamon; set aside. In a large bowl, beat butter and sugar until crumbly, about 2 minutes. Add egg and vanilla; mix well. Combine the flour, baking powder, baking soda and salt; add to butter mixture alternately with yogurt, beating just until the ingredients are combined.

Spread half of the batter evenly into a 9-in. square baking pan coated with cooking spray; sprinkle with half of the reserved sugar mixture. Repeat layers; cut through batter with a knife to swirl. Sprinkle with nuts.

Bake at 350° for 25-30 minutes or until a toothpick inserted near the center comes out clean. Cool for 5 minutes on a wire rack. Serve warm.

COFFEE LOVER'S COFFEE CAKE

NO-FRY DOUGHNUTS

NO-FRY DOUGHNUTS
YIELD: 2 DOZEN

We have four boys, and these doughnuts never last long at our house. I like them because I don't have to clean up a greasy mess after making a batch on the weekend.

susie baldwin | columbia, tennessee

2	packages (1/4 ounce *each*) active dry yeast
1/4	cup warm water (110° to 115°)
1-1/2	cups warm milk (110° to 115°)
1/3	cup shortening
1/2	cup sugar
2	eggs
1	teaspoon salt
1	teaspoon ground nutmeg
1/4	teaspoon ground cinnamon
4-1/2	to 5 cups all-purpose flour
1/4	cup butter, melted

GLAZE:

1/2	cup butter
2	cups confectioners' sugar
5	teaspoons water
2	teaspoons vanilla extract

In a large bowl, dissolve yeast in water. Add the milk and shortening; stir for 1 minute. Add sugar, eggs, salt, nutmeg, cinnamon and 2 cups flour; beat on low speed until smooth. Stir in enough remaining flour to form a soft dough (do not knead). Cover and let rise in a warm place until doubled, about 1 hour.

Punch dough down. Turn onto a floured surface; roll out to 1/2-in. thickness. Cut with a 2-3/4-in. doughnut cutter; place 2 in. apart on greased baking sheets. Brush with butter. Cover dough and let rise in a warm place until doubled, about 30 minutes.

Bake at 350° for 20 minutes or until lightly browned. Meanwhile, for glaze, melt butter in a saucepan. Add the confectioners' sugar, water and vanilla; cook over low heat until smooth (do not boil). Keep warm. Dip warm doughnuts, one at a time, into glaze and turn to coat. Drain on a wire rack. Serve immediately.

GENERAL RECIPE INDEX

ALPHABETICAL RECIPE INDEX